THE ROSARY:
"The Little Summa"

Other books by Robert Feeney

MOTHER OF THE AMERICAS

A CATHOLIC PERSPECTIVE:
PHYSICAL EXERCISE AND SPORTS

THE ROSARY:
"The Little Summa"

Robert Feeney

Third Edition, Expanded and Revised

AQUINAS
PRESS

IMPRIMATUR: ✝ Sean O'Malley, O.F.M., Cap.
Bishop of Fall River
June 6, 2001

The nihil obstat and imprimatur are official declarations that a book or pamphlet is free from doctrinal or moral error. No implication is contained therein that those who grant the nihil obstat or imprimatur agree with the contents or statements expressed.

Scripture quotations are from the Revised Standard Version Bible, Catholic Edition, Copyright 1965 and 1966 by the Division of Christian Education of the National Council of the Churches of Christ in the U.S.A. and used by permission.

Excerpts from the Jerusalem Bible, copyright © 1966 by Darton, Longman & Todd, Ltd. and Doubleday, a division of Bantam Doubleday Dell Publishing Group, Inc. Reprinted by permission

Cover photo by Arturo Mari, L'OSSERVATORE ROMANO
Photo credits: Papal pictures - Photo Service, L'OSSERVATORE ROMANO
Copyright © 1991, 1993, 1995, 1997, 2001 by Robert Feeney
First Printing.....December, 1991
Second Printing.....January, 1993, revised
Third Printing.....November 1993
Fourth Printing.....May, 1995
Fifth Printing.....February, 1997, expanded and completely revised
Sixth Printing.....July, 2001, expanded and revised

Printed in the United States of America
All rights reserved
ISBN 0-9622347-6-1
Library of Congress Control Number 2001 123598

Dedicated to Mary, Queen of the Holy Rosary,
with sincere gratitude.

Acknowledgments

Special appreciation goes to J. Francis Cardinal Stafford for his Foreword. Thanks go to those who gave their endorsements: Francis Cardinal George, O.M.I., Edward Cardinal Egan, Anthony Cardinal Bevilacqua, Adam Cardinal Maida, Theodore Cardinal McCarrick, Archbishop Gabriel Montalvo, Archbishop Elden Curtiss, Archbishop Charles Chaput, O.F.M.Cap., Bishop Paul S. Loverde, Bishop Sean O'Malley, O.F.M.Cap., Bishop Fabian Bruskewitz, Bishop John Myers, Bishop Thomas Daily, Bishop James Sullivan and Dominican Father Romanus Cessario. Thanks also to the Daughters of St. Paul, Boston, MA, for permission to quote from their books, *The Rosary* and *The Sixteen Documents of Vatican II*.

Contents

Prefatory Notes

In his *Summa Theologiae*, St. Thomas Aquinas occasionally contrasts our speculative understanding of God and our lived experience of His Grace. The Rosary, like a "little Summa," brings both of these together in a way that has sustained unity with God for centuries. Our gratitude for the Rosary is increased by the use of Robert Feeney's book, which deepens our understanding of the mysteries of Jesus' and Mary's lives and helps us participate in them by relating them to the virtues which protect and strengthen our life with God. This is a good book that will help us live faithfully.

✝ Francis Cardinal George, O.M.I.
Archbishop of Chicago

I highly recommend Robert Feeney's *The Rosary: The "Little Summa."* By drawing deeply from the wellsprings of Sacred Scripture, the Angelic Doctor, the Second Vatican Council, and Pope John Paul II, Mr. Feeney provides a vibrant background for each of the mysteries of the Rosary. The daily recitation of the Rosary is a staple of the devout life. With his book in hand, one is provided with a multiple of valuable insights for a deeper understanding of the events of Our Lord's life and the role of His Blessed Mother.

✝ Edward Cardinal Egan
Archbishop of New York

The book by Robert Feeney entitled, *The Rosary: "The Little Summa,"* offers a wonderful opportunity for all of the faithful to increase their devotion to Christ by prayerful recitation of the Most Holy Rosary. It contains rich images and develops excellent points of meditation. This book is valuable spiritual reading that will certainly inspire those who are sincere in their desire to grow in their relationship with the Lord Jesus and Mary, His Holy Mother.

✝ Anthony Cardinal Bevilacqua
Archbishop of Philadelphia

"As one who prays the rosary daily, I have found *The Rosary: "The Little Summa"* to be a wonderful guide for personal meditation and prayer. In his new third edition, Mr. Feeney offers spiritual reflections on the rosary taken from the sacred Scripture, St. Thomas Aquinas, the documents of the Second Vatican Council, the writings of the Holy Father and the *Catechism of the Catholic Church*. It is my hope that those who regularly pray the rosary as well as those who are just discovering this spiritual treasure of the Church's devotional life will find *The Rosary: "The Little Summa"* a means to deepening their relationship with Jesus through His Blessed Mother."

✝ Adam Cardinal Maida
Archbishop of Detroit

By praying the Rosary we join in Mary's own prayer as she leads us through the mysteries of Christ's life–His incarnation, passion, death, resurrection and glory–and in this way helps us to be configured to Him. I am happy to commend this third edition of Robert Feeney's *The Rosary: "The Little Summa"* to readers to seek a deeper understanding of the mysteries and an aid to more prayerful recitation of the Rosary.

✝ Theodore Cardinal McCarrick
Archbishop of Washington

This collection of beautiful and inspiring meditations on the mysteries of the Rosary is spiritual food for the faithful. I hope and pray that this book will bring a new generation of seekers to Jesus Christ through Mary, Mother of God and Mother of the Church.

✝ J. Francis Cardinal Stafford
President of the Pontifical
Council for the Laity
Rome, Italy

Many can remember learning to pray the Rosary as little children, while others may have discovered this treasure later in life. For more than four centuries this exquisite and powerful prayer has lead countless souls to Jesus, through the heart of the Virgin Mary. Now, Mr. Feeney's book, *The Rosary: "The Little Summa"*, can be a source of instruction and an aid in meditation for those who wish to deepen their understanding and appreciation of the Rosary as a true and efficacious prayer in the life of the Church.

✝ Gabriel Montalvo
Apostolic Nuncio to the United States

As scaffolding surrounds and supports the construction of a building, so Robert Feeney's *The Rosary: "The Little Summa"* provides important foundation and inspiration for the prayerful recitation of the Rosary. The meditation and study helps from authoritative sources will benefit anyone who takes them to heart and to prayer.

✝ Elden Curtiss
Archbishop of Omaha

May God bless Robert Feeney for a delightful set of reflections: they can only lead us closer to Jesus and His mother. A wonderful book.

✝ Charles J. Chaput, O.F.M., Cap.
Archbishop of Denver

As the Church passes into the Third Christian Millennium, our Holy Father, Pope John Paul II, recalls the need for Christians to grow daily in sanctity. He writes, "This training in holiness calls for a Christian life distinguished above all in the art of prayer."

One of the greatest prayers the Church possesses is the Rosary. This third edition of Robert Feeney's book, entitled *The Rosary: "The Little Summa"*, beautifully develops the heart of each mystery of the Rosary in light of the teachings of the saints, the Second Vatical Council, and the mind of Pope John Paul II.

May this book be an inspiration for all who read it to deepen their life of prayer in union with Mary, our Blessed Mother, that she in turn may lead them ever closer to Christ Jesus, her Son.

✝ Paul S. Loverde
Bishop of Arlington

Robert Feeney's *The Rosary: "The Little Summa"* is an excellent treatise for people seeking a deeper understanding and appreciation of this beautiful prayer. He has combined Scripture, the writings of Thomas Aquinas, and Church teachings in his exposition of the Mysteries of the Rosary. His reflections will certainly afford the reader ample material for meditation, which is the soul of the Rosary.

✝ Sean O'Malley, O.F.M.Cap.
Bishop of Fall River

The Rosary, "The Little Summa" contains the wisdom and teaching of St. Thomas Aquinas and numerous other Saints, Doctors, and Popes of the Church. It truly captures the tradition of the Church on the subject of the Rosary. Robert Feeney combines history with spiritual insight to offer a rich source for both intellectual knowledge and deeper prayer.

✠ Fabian W. Bruskewitz
Bishop of Lincoln

The Second Vatican Council has called all men and women to renewed commitment to personal holiness. Both Paul VI in his apostolic exhortation *Marialis Cultus* and John Paul II in his post-synod exhortation *Familiaris Consortio* have recommended the Rosary as a particularly excellent way for individuals and the family to grow closer to Jesus Christ and His Church. By meditating on the various mysteries of the Rosary one meditates on the life of Our Lord with particular emphasis on the role of Our Lady in salvation history. It is indeed a "little summa" of the basic *kerygma* of the Christian faith.

I would highly recommend the daily recitation of the Rosary to anyone seriously interested in their spiritual life. Mr. Feeney's book is an excellent introduction to the Rosary, its mysteries and its importance in the spiritual life.

✠ John J. Myers
Bishop of Peoria

I have found *The Rosary: "The Little Summa"* to be an excellent boost to daily prayer and devotion to Our Lady according to the mind of our Holy Father Pope John Paul II. Many people will benefit from this book.

✠ James S. Sullivan
Bishop of Fargo
President of the World
Apostolate of Fatima

In *The Rosary: "The Little Summa,"* we are offered enlightening and thought-provoking insights into two of the Church's great treasures - the Rosary and the thought of St. Thomas Aquinas. The reader will certainly be drawn closer to Our Lord and His Blessed Mother.

✠ Thomas V. Daily
Bishop of Brooklyn

Our Lady's Rosary occupies a unique place in the Church's treasury of devotions. Thanks to the efforts of Robert Feeney, those who wish to enrich their meditation on the 15 decades now possess a helpful aid. I highly recommend this book to those for whom a faithful recitation of the Rosary forms an integral part of their prayer and devotion.

Romanus Cessario, O.P.
Professor of Theology
St. John's School of Theology
Brighton, MA

Foreword

THIS THIRD EDITION has new material including a chapter entitled, "John Paul II: The Rosary, My Favorite Prayer." One readily understands why the Pope chose the rosary as his 'favorite prayer.' Other Christians have made the same judgement. In fact, its title underlines its popularity. Meaning *A Garden of Roses*, its name captures the experience of praying the rosary. It is like a spiritual sojourn in a rose-garden. Over the centuries millions have found delight and wisdom in using it for prayer.

In an old liturgical hymn on the rosary, the Church sings, "Come, nations of the world, gather flowers from this rose-garden of mysteries, and weave rose-garlands for her who gave birth to all noble love." This verse expresses its universal and grass-roots appeal.

The rose-flower is the origin of its name. A rose has distinctive characteristics - its visual beauty, its fragrance and the softness of its petals. Other forms of prayer also associate Mary's glory with the rose-flower. In the Litany of Loretto Our Lady is invoked as *Mystical Rose*. In Dante's *Paradise* the ranks of angels and saints take the form of a white rose with its many layers of petals and the Virgin Mary in the first rank. The great windows of French Gothic Cathedrals are shaped like a rose. From the earliest pilgrimage of my priestly ministry, I have never forgotten the central subject of the rose-window above the north porch of the Cathedral of Chartres: Mary holding her Son surrounded by four doves and eight angels (13th c.).

Others have walked through this mystical rose-garden. The Flemish painter, Jan van Eyck, in his *Madonna at the Fountain* (1439 AD), shows Mary embracing the Child Jesus in an enclosed rose-garden before a delicate fountain. He employs ancient imagery to portray God-among-us and the paradise he has prepared for us. In his Commentary on the *Canticle of Canticles*, Rupert of Deutz (c.

1070-1129) identified Mary not only as the garden, but also as the fountain of gardens recalling the bride's role in the fourth chapter of the *Canticle*. The title's antecedents are ancient and rich.

The rosary engages all the mystical sensibilities of Christians. St. Augustine, writing of the experience of God in prayer, described these spiritual senses, "There my soul receives a radiance that no space can grasp; there something resounds which no time can take away; there something gives a fragrance which no wind can dissipate; there something is savored which no satiety can make bitter; there something is embraced which can occasion no ennui."

Like the rose-flower, the graces of the rosary engage the spiritual senses. They include the spiritual 'fragrance,' the gentle 'sense of touch' and the 'visual' attractiveness of the 15 mysteries of Jesus and Mary. In praying the rosary our deepest interiority is engaged. In contemplating Jesus through the maternal eyes of Mary we sense his presence as a light and a touch and a fragrance. For in loving Jesus we love One who is light and fragrance and embrace to the interior person.

The spiritual sense of touch is especially important in prayer to Mary. Our Blessed Mother is reported to have said many centuries ago, "Let me tell you that when you greet me with the Angelical Salutation, I experience a great thrill of joy and more especially when you utter lingeringly the words *The Lord is with you*. The delight I feel then is more than can be expressed in words. For then it seems to me that I feel my Son within me even as He, true God and true man, was with me when he vouchsafed to be born of me for the sake of sinners."

Hans Urs von Balthasar, a great theologian of the 20th century, elaborates on Mary's blind sense of touch while carrying Jesus within her womb. The unique maternal touch is the fundamental unerring sense. "[While carrying the child within her womb] the mother is still both herself and her child. And her feeling of the child still wholly encompasses within herself being felt by the child - just as the believer's vision of God presupposes his being seen by God. Seen in the light of Mary's simple experience of motherhood, which in her has become a function of the archetypal act of faith, all closed consciousness of self and all closed experience of self becomes problematic: the experience of self must open out, through faith, to an experience that encompasses oneself and the other - oneself and the burgeoning Word of God, which at first seems to be growing in the self until in this growth it becomes evident that it is the self that is contained in the Word of God."

Further surprise and wonder await those who pray the mysteries of the rosary. Gardens of flowers have been associated with historic dramas: those enacted in the Garden of Eden, in the enclosed garden of the Canticle of Canticles and in the garden near Golgotha "in which there was a new tomb." On a fresco in the interior of the *Porziuncula* chapel, St. Francis of Assisi is seen presenting Jesus and Mary with a crown of red and white roses from the gardens near S. Maria of the Angels, indicating that he had experienced the double initiation of divine love (the red roses) and divine wisdom (white roses).

One walks through the mystical rose-garden of the rosary and one's heart is amazed by the drama unfolding there. Through the maternal eyes of Mary we experience again the overwhelming newness of the Christian reality.

The drama of Jesus of Nazareth and of Mary of Nazareth is the primordial drama of divine and human freedoms. In the Joyful Mysteries, Mary's drama of faith begins with her creative receptivity to the gift of God's grace. She was totally open to the Archangel Gabriel's announcement of God's word to her. In her *fiat (Be it done to me according to your word),* she accepted all that followed in the Sorrowful Mysteries. In the final part of the threefold garland, the Glorious Mysteries, the revelation of God reaches its consummation: the Word which comes from God returns to God, bearing all of creation with Him. "In the bodily and spiritual glory which she possesses in heaven, the Mother of Jesus continues in this present world as the image and first flowering of the Church as she is to be perfected in the world to come" (*Lumen Gentium 67*).

Each of us is caught up in this drama of freedom. The experience of salvation does not originate from ourselves but from God. "But to all who received him, who believed in his name, he gave power to become children of God; who were born, not of blood, nor of the will of the flesh, nor of the will of man, but of God" (Jn 1:12-13).

The author of the Christian drama is God. "We love, because he first loved us" (1 Jn. 4:19). God reveals his love in the Paschal Mystery. God first offers to *impress* Jesus's kenotic [self-emptying] form upon the individual through word and sacrament. Like Mary, the believer freely accepts the divine 'impression' and begins to give external witness to Christ. The Christian *expresses* the mystery of Jesus externally through witness to him in everyday word and deed.

The rosary follows the same pattern. From the power of God's word *impressing* itself upon us in the mysteries of the rosary, the revelation is received, is apprehended and then is *expressed* through our witness to Christ in marriage, families, parishes, schools, work, politics, economics, labor unions, etc.

Praying the rosary helps us to have the mind among ourselves which is ours in Christ Jesus (Phil 2:5). He emptied himself for our sake; he humbled himself for our salvation even to accepting death, death upon the Cross. The rosary leads us to 'the same instinct of obedience' which guided Jesus throughout his life, and especially when his 'hour' had come. For he said, "My food is to do the will of him who sent me (Jn. 4:34). May many more persons taste the divine wisdom found in this extraordinary garden.

✝ J. Francis Cardinal Stafford
President, Pontifical Council for the Laity

Chapter 1

The Papal Tradition

IT CAN BE SAID that the whole history of the Rosary may be learned in papal decrees, bulls and encyclicals. The papal tradition of the Rosary is singled out in decrees, bulls and encyclicals written by Popes starting with Pope Urban IV and ending with Pope Leo XIII. Pope Leo XIII finished and crowned the papal tradition concerning the Rosary in the early 20th century. The papal tradition stands out by itself. It is made by the Popes alone. The bulls of Leo X, St. Pius V, Sixtus V and the encyclicals of Leo XIII give the history of the Rosary a marvelous degree of fullness.

It seems as if the Popes, who are guardians of Catholic tradition, had looked into all the histories and had extracted the truth about the Rosary from the various legends and facts mixed together. Papal tradition, in this regard, is based on a method of selection and discrimination. The Popes, in regards to the Rosary tradition, are superior to secular historians. They are guided by the Holy Spirit and have the gift of speaking with the highest authority.

Papal decrees, bulls and encyclicals have authority in the historical sphere. The Popes are head of the Vatican Library. They have learned men assist them in the composition of decrees, bulls and encyclicals. Popes do not accept facts without reasonable proofs. The facts go through tests of research and verification before they are officially approved. The tradition of the Rosary is what it is because the Popes have made it so.

Pope Leo X in *Pastoris Aeterni* (1520) attributed the institution of the Rosary to St. Dominic. The Dominican Pope, St. Pius V, stated fifty years later in *Consueverunt Romani Pontifices*, September 15, 1569, the following:

> "The Albigensian heresy, then raging in a part of France, had blinded so many of the laity that they were cruelly attacking priests and clerics. Blessed Dominic lifted his eyes to heaven and turned them toward the Virgin Mary, the Mother of God. Dominic invented this method of prayer, which is easy and suitable to everyone and which is called the Rosary.
>
> "It consists of venerating the Blessed Virgin by reciting one hundred and fifty angelic salutations, the same number as the Psalms of David, interrupting them at each decade by the Lord's Prayer, meanwhile meditating on the mysteries, which recall the entire life of our Lord Jesus Christ. After having devised it Dominic and his sons spread this form of prayer throughout the Church."[1]

The tradition of St. Dominic and the Rosary was universally excepted until the time of the Bollandists in the 17th century. The Bollandists were a group of Belgian Jesuits who, under the direction of John Bolland in 1630, worked on publishing the *Acta Sanctorium*, covering the life of Christ and of the saints included in the liturgical calendar. They were to rewrite the lives of the saints based on historical evidence. The Bollandists concluded that there was not enough evidence to support the tradition of St. Dominic and the Rosary. The Popes coming after the Bollandists did not accept this claim and rejected the Bollandists' research.

A century after the Bollandists, in 1724, Pope Benedict XIII asked Cardinal Prospero Lambertini, Promoter of the Faith at that time, to look into the tradition of St. Dominic and the Rosary. Cardinal Lambertini was a scholar and promoter of historical studies and research when with the Congregation of Sacred Rites. The Cardinal thoroughly investigated the research and affirmed the tradition of St.

Pope St. Pius V, one of the great Rosary Popes,
is buried here in St. Mary Major Basilica in Rome.

Dominic being the true author of the Rosary. His conclusions were accepted by Pope Benedict XIII. As Archbishop of Bologna, Italy, the Cardinal would visit St. Dominic's tomb in the Basilica of St. Dominic in Bologna once a week. As Archbishop of Bologna, he had published a work which spoke of St. Dominic:

> "The Popes in their decrees, to which assent is to be given, rightly designated St. Dominic as the author and institutor of the Rosary. St. Dominic had given a crushing blow to the dread errors of the Albigensians by means of this divine safeguard of the Rosary (Institut. Ecclesiast., Instit. 79, num. 12)."

In other published works, Cardinal Lambertini was so convincing in showing St. Dominic's connection with the Rosary that a rigorous critic named Baillet stated:

> "It was wrong and unjust to wrest that glory from St. Dominic."

Afterwards, Cardinal Lambertini would soon become Pope Benedict XIV (1740-58). As Pope he was asked about St. Dominic's connection with the Rosary. He responded:

> "You ask whether St. Dominic was the first institutor of the Rosary and show that you yourselves are bewildered and entangled in doubts on the matter. Now what value do you attach to the testimony of so many Popes, such as Leo X (1521), Pius V (1572), Gregory XIII (1585), Sixtus V (1590), Clement VIII (1605), Alexander VII (1667), B. Innocent XI (1689), Clement XI (1721), Innocent XIII (1724) and others who unanimously attribute the institution of the Rosary to St. Dominic".[2]

In his investigation of the Rosary tradition, Pope Benedict XIV referred to the will of Anthony Ser, dated 1221. In this will, Anthony

*The papal tradition affirms that St. Dominic
is the true author of the Rosary.*

Ser wrote:

> "I bequeath money to the Confraternity of the Rosary founded by the good Dominic Guzman, of which I am a member."[3]

This is a proof that the Rosary existed in the 13th century and was founded by St. Dominic.

The Dominican tradition of the Rosary was endorsed by Pope Benedict XIV and the Holy See. The papal tradition supports the Dominican tradition, which is summarized in the words of P. Cornelius de Snecka, O.P., a disciple of the Dominican Alan de la Roche:

> "We read that at the time when he was preaching to the Albigensians, St. Dominic at first obtained, but scanty success; and that one day, complaining of this in pious prayer to Our Blessed Lady, she deigned to reply:
>
> 'Wonder not until now thou hast gathered so little fruit from thy labors; thou hast spent them on a barren soil, not yet watered with the dew of Divine Grace. When God willed to renew the face of the earth, He began by sending down the fertilizing rain of the Angelic Salutation. Therefore, preach my Psalter, composed of 150 Angelic Salutations and 15 Our Fathers, and thou wilt obtain an abundant harvest.' The servant of God in consequence began to preach this devotion and make it known to the people, and from that moment, he gathered in an immense harvest of souls (Sermon 10., Sup. Conf. De Serto Rosario)."[4]

The recently made Blessed, Pope Pius IX, in his letter *Egregus suis*, December 3, 1869, stated:

> "As St. Dominic employed this prayer as a sword to destroy the monstrous heresy of the Albigenses, so

likewise in our time the Faithful, in using the same weapon–that is to say, the daily recitation of the Rosary–will obtain that, by the all-powerful protection of the Mother of God, the many errors infecting the world will be uprooted and destroyed."[5]

Blessed Pope Pius IX also in a letter *C'est un fiat e'clatant* on February 8, 1875, wrote:

"As you know, dear Sons, it is a celebrated fact that the Rosary was entrusted by the Holy Mother of God to St. Dominic as a singular help when he battled against monstrous errors."[6]

Pope Leo XIII, in his 12 encyclicals on the Rosary, written over a period of 20 years, describes St. Dominic as the founder of the Rosary. In his encyclicals, we find a complete summary of everything that previous Popes had declared about St. Dominic being the founder. Pope Leo XIII constantly put forward St. Dominic as the founder of both the Rosary and the Confraternity of the Rosary. In his encyclicals, Leo XIII reminds us of the depth of gratitude we owe St. Dominic. In his encyclical *Supremi Apostolatus*, September 1, 1883, he states:

"As you know, God in His mercy, raised up against the Albigenses a most holy man, the illustrious Father and Founder of the Dominican Order. He undauntedly proceeded to attack the enemies of the Catholic Church, not by force of arms, but by the devotion which he was the first to institute under the name of the Holy Rosary. St. Dominic composed the Rosary in such a way that the mysteries of our salvation are recalled to mind in succession. This method of meditation is interspersed and, as it were, interlaced with the Hail Mary and with the prayer to God, the Father of our Lord Jesus Christ."[7]

Pope Leo XIII, Pope of the Rosary,
is buried here in St. John Lateran Basilica in Rome.

Again, in his decree for the Proper Office for Rosary Sunday (August 5, 1888), Leo XIII wrote:

> "Our need for Divine Help is certainly no less today than when the great Dominic preached the Rosary of Mary as a remedy to heal the wounds of Christendom. This great saint composed the formula of the Rosary having for its end the meditations on the mysteries of salvation combined with a recitation of a connected chain of the "Hail Mary" and with the occasional introduction of the "Our Father."[8]

This great Rosary Pope stated in the encyclical *Octobri mense*, September 22, 1891, the following:

> "It was at Mary's prompting and suggesting that the famous St. Dominic introduced and propagated the Rosary as a powerful weapon against the enemies of the faith in an era that was very hostile to Catholicism quite like our era."[9]

Leo XIII in his encyclical *Magnal Dei Matris*, September 7, 1892, states:

> "The Mother of God taught the Rosary to the patriarch Dominic in order that he might propagate it."[10]

It was on June 29, 1921, that Pope Benedict XV in this encyclical *Fausto appetente die* stated:

> "How gratifying to the Queen of heaven was the devotion of St. Dominic is seen from the fact that she made use of him to teach the Church, the Spouse of her Son, the Most Holy Rosary. This is a form of prayer which combines the use of mind as well as

lips; for in it we contemplate the principle mysteries of religion while at the same time repeating the 'Our Father' fifteen times, and the fifteen decades of 'Hail Mary's.' Hence, it is well calculated to stir up devotion and nourish all virtues among God's people."[11]

In his letter *Inclytam ac perilustrem*, March 6, 1934, Pope Pius XI stated:

> "Among the weapons St. Dominic used to convert the heretics, the most efficacious, as the faithful well know, was the Marian Rosary, the practice of which, taught by the Blessed Virgin herself, has so widely been spread throughout the Catholic world. Now where does the efficacy and power of this manner of praying come from? Certainly from the mysteries of the Divine Redeemer which we contemplate and piously meditate on."[12]

In conclusion, the Church, through her Popes, has given us this papal tradition of the true origin and history of the Rosary. This papal tradition is declared in no less than 214 papal bulls, decrees and encyclicals of no fewer than 39 Popes.

St. Dominic: Herald of the Rosary

Chapter 2

St. Dominic and the Rosary

W HO IS ST. DOMINIC, the one to whom the Church, through her Popes, has honored down through the centuries as the author of the Rosary?

Dominic Guzman was born in 1170 in the town of Caleruega in Castile, the north-central region of Spain. He was born of devout and reputable parents, Felix and Jane. His father was a honorable man, a member of the rural knighthood and having considerable property in his town. His mother, Jane, was from Aza, nineteen miles from Caleruega. She was a most merciful woman, full of compassion for the unfortunate and afflicted. She was beatified by Pope Leo XII in 1828.

Jane had two sons, Mannes and Anthony. She had gone to the nearby Abbey of Silos to pray for another son. She prayed to St. Dominic of Silos to intercede with God in this matter. She had a vision of this great saint who said:

> "My daughter, your prayers are heard and God will
> send you a son. He will be a great servant of God and
> do mighty deeds for Christ and the Church."[1]

Before the birth of little Dominic, Jane had a prophetic dream in which she beheld her son as a black and white dog running about with a lighted torch in its jaws, setting the world aflame. This was to signify that her child would be an eminent preacher.

*Blessed Jane went to the Abbey of Silos to pray for
another son. St. Dominic of Silos appeared to her in a vision
and said: "God will send you a son."*

When little Dominic was baptized in the parish church, his grand-mother saw a bright shining light, like a star on his brow. This was to signify that he was destined to be a light, one who would illumine those who sit in darkness. In the Dialogue of St. Catherine of Siena, Catherine states that God revealed to her:

> "He (Dominic) took up the task of the Word, my only begotten Son. Clearly he appeared as an apostle in the world with such truth and light did he sow my word, dispelling the darkness and giving light. He was a light that I offered the world through Mary."[2]

His father, Felix, was a fighting man, a knight who carried a sword against the Moors. This characteristic would leave its stamp on Dominic in fighting for the faith and against error. We owe to his mother, Jane, the fortune that placed a book in Dominic's hand instead of a sword.

His mother had a profound influence on Dominic. Devotion to Mary given by St. Dominic to his spiritual children comes from one source, his own mother. The print of her personality will be seen for all time on the Order founded by her son. He learned the value of combining vocal and mental prayer from her. His mother would tell him little stories of the life of Jesus that he would come to know as mysteries and which he would one day come to preach.

From age 7 to 14, Dominic went to live with his uncle, the priest of the church of Gumiel d'Izan, a town about twenty miles northwest of Caleruega. Under the care of his uncle, his mother's brother, Dominic began his first studies. He then went on to study rhetoric, philosophy, natural science, theology and Sacred Scripture at the University of Palencia. His course of studies at the university lasted ten years, six of which were devoted to the arts and four to theology. He was always radiant and joyous, except when moved by some misfortune of his neighbors. His appearance was attractive and his voice had a loud, rich and full sound to it like a sonorous bell.

He was ordained a priest at age 24. The Bishop of Osma, Martin

St. Dominic was born in 1170 in Caleruega, Castile,
the north-central region of Spain.
The water well, below, is the site of his birth.

de Bazan, summoned Dominic to his Cathedral and made him a canon regular of St. Augustine. He served as a canon for nine years. He began to shine as a special star among the canons. His eyes gleamed and his mind and will were in perfect harmony. Dominic lived the rule of St. Augustine and chanted the Divine Office with the other canons. He prayed and wept for sinners and the afflicted. He felt the sufferings of others and had compassion for them with his merciful heart. He loved to read the book *Conferences of the Fathers of the Desert* by John Cassian.

Dominic became Prior at the age of 31. All during this time in Osma, God was forming his character, training him as an athlete of Christ and preparing him for the life of a preacher. Sister Cecilia, who would come to know Dominic well, described him as being of middle height with a handsome face and a slightly ruddy complexion. His hair and beard were fair and a certain radiance came from his forehead which attracted many to love and respect him. He had long hands and a strong voice. He never went bald, but a few white hairs of age began to appear. Dominic left Osma in 1203 at the age of 33 and took up preaching in an area of southern France called *Languedoc*. It was during this time of preaching in *Languedoc* that Mary revealed the Rosary to St. Dominic.

The origin of the Rosary is rooted in the 13th century. At that time, France was threatened by the Albigensian heresy with roots centuries old. Its roots go back to early Christianity as it was basically the Manichean heresy of St. Augustine's time. The Albigensians believed that all life on earth–being the work of Satan–was evil. This belief in the essential evil of matter led to a terrible system of murder. Marriage was considered a crime and suicide was considered praiseworthy since it put an end to the existence of matter. The Albigensians anti-life attitude produced a culture of death. They had no respect for the dignity of human life. They totally renounced the teachings of the Catholic Church. After much fruitless labor preaching to the Albigensians, tradition has it that in the year 1208, the revelation of the Rosary to St. Dominic took place in the Chapel of

*St. Dominic spent 9 years as a canon regular at the Cathedral
(above) in Osma, Spain.
The choir stall (below) was St. Dominic's.*

St. Mary at Prouille in southern France. St. Dominic was praying and tearfully complaining to the Mother of God about the poor fruits of his preaching to the Albigensians. In the midst of his lament the Mother of God appeared to him and said:

> "Wonder not that until now you have obtained so little fruit by your labors: you have spent them on a barren soil, not yet watered with the dew of divine grace. When God willed to renew the face of the earth, He began by sending down on it the fertilizing rain of the Angelic Salutation. Preach my Psalter (rosary) composed of 150 Angelic Salutations and 15 Our Fathers and you will obtain an abundant harvest."[3]

Now that Mary had revealed to St. Dominic that "the earth will remain barren till watered by this heavenly dew," he wasted no time.

Pope Benedict XIII, himself a Dominican, in 1726, in a decree stated:

> "St. Dominic received a command from the Queen of heaven to preach the Rosary to the people as a singular remedy against error and vice."

Both Leo XIII and Pius XI accepted the Chapel of St. Mary at Prouille in southern France as the place where St. Dominic received the revelation of the Rosary. Pius XI in *Ingravescentibus malis* (Sept. 29, 1937), stated:

> "Prouille was the cradle of the Rosary."

After Mary's revelation to him, St. Dominic went straight to the town of Toulouse, not far from Prouille, where the people gathered there in the church. St. Louis de Montfort so wonderfully states in his book *Secret of the Rosary*:

> "So fervently and compellingly did he explain the importance and value of the Holy Rosary, that almost all the people of Toulouse embraced it and renounced

The revelation of the Rosary was given to St. Dominic in the
Chapel of St. Mary at Prouille in southern France.
Pius XI stated: "Prouille was the cradle of the Rosary."

their false beliefs. In a very short time a great
improvement was seen in the town; people began leading
Christian lives and gave up their former bad habits."[4]

It is said of St. Dominic that he would go from town to town and
preach. In his travels he showed tremendous physical endurance.
His slim figure retained its youthful litheness and flexibility under
all the physical efforts of travel. He would preach on the Gospel
truths that centered on the joyful, sorrowful and glorious life of Christ.
He would invite his hearers to pick up the beads and pray the Our
Father and Hail Mary only after he mentioned a mystery and gave a
sermon on a phase of Jesus' life.

St. Dominic has the honor of being the author of the Rosary, though
he did not compose the Rosary in its definitive form that we have
today. The fixing of definite mysteries was a long process which
took centuries to evolve and determine. That was done by Pope St.
Pius V, himself a Dominican, in 1569. This great Pope of the Rosary
set into place the fifteen mysteries that we meditate on today. Since
it is the seed that counts, without it, there would be neither rosebush
nor roses, so too without the apostolic genius and holiness of St.
Dominic we would not have had the Rosary that has developed slowly
throughout the centuries.

A past Dominican Master General, Martin Gillet, O.P., in his letter
to all Dominicans on the subject of the Rosary, mentioned that the
Albigensians were ignorant of Christian teaching. They only knew
the Our Father and Hail Mary. He stated in his letter that St. Dominic
taught the people the Gospel by taking the only remaining elements
of faith they still had–the Our Father and Hail Mary. St. Dominic
introduced order in saying these prayers by breaking up the Hail Marys
into decades, each decade preceded by the Our Father and each decade preceded by an event of Christ's life taken from the Gospel. By
means of the life story of Jesus, preached and prayed in the mysteries
of the Rosary, Dominic taught the great truths of salvation. He took
the people hand in hand with Mary through the events of the life of
her Son. St. Dominic's use of the Rosary was, what Pope Paul VI

would come to call, a "Gospel prayer."

In regards to the beads or string of knots that St. Dominic used for the praying of the prayers–the deceased English Dominican Bede Jarrett in his book on St. Dominic mentions that papal tradition points to St. Dominic as the originator of decades or groups of ten Hail Marys separated by a larger bead, the Our Father.

The word Rosary was not used during Dominic's time. It was referred to as the Psalter of Mary. The word Rosary was given to it much later. St. Louis De Montfort in his classic *Secret of the Rosary* states that ever since Alan de la Roche, O.P., reestablished the Rosary in 1460, the people started using the word Rosary. According to some writers the Rosary takes its name from the Latin word *ros*, which means dew. This may be accounted for by Mary's words to St. Dominic:

> "Until now, you have spent thy labors on barren soil,
> not yet watered with the dew of divine grace."

Other writers trace the adoption of the word Rosary to the Latin word *rosarium,* which means a crown of roses. The deceased Dominican Cardinal Luigi Ciappi, O.P., wrote that St. Dominic can be regarded as the ardent promoter of the Psalter of Mary which later was called the Rosary. Cardinal Ciappi, O.P., who was a theologian, wrote that St. Dominic preached the mysteries of the life, death and resurrection of Christ, alternating with the prayers the Our Father and Hail Mary.

St. Dominic meditated on the mysteries of the Faith found in the Gospel. From the abundance and fullness of contemplation that flowed from his meditating on the life, death and resurrection of Jesus, Dominic taught the people. We think of St. Dominic sitting and meditating on the Gospels as he is so doing in the picture at the beginning of this chapter. He followed the example of Mary, pondering the mysteries of her Son in her heart. He gives us an example to help us meditate with Mary on the mysteries of her Son found in the mysteries of the Rosary. His example can help us experience meditation that can lead to contemplation and, eventually, expand into the apostolate.

St. Louis de Montfort wrote that the Rosary was St. Dominic's preparation for every sermon. He wrote that when Dominic preached the Rosary, he would speak in the simplicity of the Holy Spirit and with His forcefulness. St. Louis stated that St. Dominic was so convinced of the Rosary, that when he heard confessions, he hardly ever gave any penance other than the Rosary.

The battle of Muret in southern France forms a part of St. Dominic's life. The King of Aragon appeared before the walls of Muret on September 10, 1213, with 40,000 Albigensian soldiers. He totally surprised Count Simon De Montfort, leader of the Catholic army. De Montfort had only 800 men. Before the battle on September 13th, 1213, the Bishop of Uzes offered Mass at the Church of St. James and Bishop Fulk of Toulouse blessed the soldiers with the relic of the true Cross.

St. Dominic was in Muret at the time. He suggested that the Rosary be prayed before the battle. While the battle raged, we are told that St. Dominic was in the Church of St. James praying the Rosary with arms extended. The soldiers and Count Simon De Montfort attributed their complete victory over the King of Aragon and his army to the Rosary. In gratitude, Simon De Montfort built the first chapel in honor of the Rosary, located in the Church of St. James in Muret, not too far from Toulouse in southern France.

In 1215, two years after the battle of Muret, St. Dominic went to Rome and appealed to Pope Innocent III for permission to found an Order of preachers to carry the Gospel truths throughout the world. The Pope directed him to adopt a rule already in existence to live by. St. Dominic and his followers unanimously chose the rule of St. Augustine. In 1216, a new Pope, Honorius III, granted full approval. He confirmed the Order of Preachers on December 23, 1216.

While St. Dominic was in Rome, God confirmed the preaching vocation of Dominic's Order. St. Peter and St. Paul appeared to Dominic while at prayer in St. Peter's Basilica. St. Peter handed him

*The first chapel (above) built in honor of the Rosary is located
in the Church of St. James (below) in Muret,
in southern France near Toulouse.*

a pilgrim staff and St. Paul gave him a book and they said:

> "Go and preach, for to this ministry you have been called."[5]

Jesus appeared to St. Dominic and declared:

> "I have given your Order over to the care of my Mother."[6]

Mary used to appear to the followers of St. Dominic and show her motherly affection for them. She would smile at them, encourage them, correct them when needed, protect them, comfort them and bless them.

In 1218, the Mother of God appeared in Rome to a Dominican named Master Reginald of Orleans. He was appointed superior by St. Dominic of the Dominicans stationed in Bologna, Italy. He was seriously ill when Mary appeared to him. She cured him and showed him a white scapular saying:

> "Behold this is the habit of your Order."[7]

More than one hundred years after the cure of Blessed Reginald, God spoke to St. Catherine of Siena, concerning Mary's choice of habit for the Dominicans:

> "He (St. Dominic) was a light which I gave to the world by means of Mary placed in the mystical body of holy Church as an extirpator of heresies. Why do I say by means of Mary? Because Mary gave him his habit–this office was committed to her by my goodness."[8]

Our Lord revealed to St. Catherine of Siena that He approved of St. Dominic's Order. Of the first Dominicans, God revealed:

> "They were like St. Paul, so enlightened that no darksome error appeared in their sight, without being

dispersed."[9]

Pope Honorius III would come to call the Dominicans: "Champions of the Faith and True Lights of the World."

St. Dominic loved the company of the young and many of those who were generous hearted were drawn to him and his new Order. He was always affectionate to everyone and very good to talk to when in trouble. He always made people feel at home when talking to him. He always consoled those who came to him in times of difficulty. He had playfulness in his character and yearly he grew more boyish, more light of heart. He was a great companion.

St. Dominic lived for five years after his Order was approved. St. Dominic was like a doctor, using the Rosary as a serum, injecting all the afflicted with it, so that vices would be rooted out and virtues infused. The Rosary was like an ointment which St. Dominic and his followers used to heal all the mutilated members of both Church and State.

St. Dominic died on August 6, 1221, in Bologna, Italy. He died in a cell which is nicely preserved today in the Priory of St. Dominic in Bologna, Italy. John Paul II visited this cell on April 19, 1982. Before he died St. Dominic said to the members of his Order:

> "Do not weep, my children, I shall be more useful
> to you where I am going than I have ever been in this
> life."[10]

During his lifetime Dominic healed the sick, raised the dead and multiplied food. His death was followed by many miracles. He is buried in the Basilica of St. Dominic also in Bologna, Italy. His beautiful white marble tomb is known as the Ark of Dominic. He was canonized by Pope Gregory IX in 1234, who is recorded as saying of St. Dominic:

> "I have no more doubt of the sanctity of this man,
> than I have of St. Peter or St. Paul."[11]

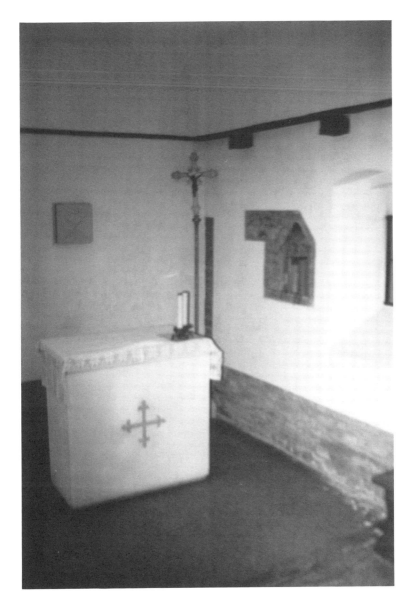

*St. Dominic died in this cell in Bologna, Italy,
on August 6, 1221. It is nicely preserved in the
Priory of St. Dominic in Bologna.*

*St. Dominic is buried in the Basilica of St. Dominic
in Bologna, Italy.
His tomb here is called the Ark of Dominic.*

After Dominic's death, Dominicans throughout the centuries have followed the example of St. Dominic using the Rosary when fighting the "isms" of their day, which, like the Albigensian heresy of St. Dominic's time, are contrary to the teachings of the Church.

The first great follower of St. Dominic to be an outstanding champion of the Rosary was Alan de la Roche, O.P. He was born in 1428 in Brittany, France. He distinguished himself in philosophy and was a Master of Theology. He lectured in Paris and wrote a commentary on the Sentences of Peter Lombard. He was a marvelous preacher and restorer of the Rosary in northern France, Flanders and the Netherlands.

This great Dominican had to reestablish devotion to the Rosary because it gradually began to be neglected after St. Dominic had instituted it. In the Breviary lessons on the Octave day of the Rosary feast during the papacy of Sixtus IV (1471-84), it is stated:

> "After the entrance of the Blessed Dominic into Heaven, the custom of saying the Rosary gradually began to be neglected, till it had almost died out, then the Most Holy Virgin appeared to Alan and admonished him that he and his brother preachers were to endeavor to restore the custom."[12]

According to his biographers, this vision of Mary was a commission similar to the one given to St. Dominic earlier. Whereas Dominic was commissioned to institute the Rosary, Alan was commissioned to reestablish it. This vision of Mary to him is assigned to the year 1460. Alan de la Roche, O.P., wrote a book entitled the *Dignity of the Rosary of the Blessed Virgin*, which treats the origins of the Rosary and St. Dominic establishing this devotion. St. Louis de Montfort refers to this book several times in his classic *Secret of the Rosary*.

All Dominicans are called by the Church to be the Dominic of their times in preaching the Rosary. It was St. Catherine of Siena who said:

"The voice of Dominic's preaching is still heard today and will continue to be heard in the preaching of his followers."[13]

Pope Leo XIII entrusted the Dominican Order with the express mission of promoting the Rosary. He stated:

"This devotion is the rightful property of the Dominican family and to the Friar Preachers is entrusted the commission to teach it to the Catholic world."

Leo XIII once told the Vicar-General of the Dominican Order in an audience granted September 26, 1883:

"Let all the children of St. Dominic rouse themselves for the conflict, and let them prepare themselves as mighty warriors to use those arms which has been provided, with such wonderful foresight by their Blessed Father, Dominic. Let them propagate the Rosary everywhere."[14]

Pope Benedict XV in his encyclical of June 29, 1921, *Fausto appetente die*, stated:

"We wish all Dominicans to make it their particular task to familiarize Christ's flock with the use of the holy Rosary."

Pope Pius XI, in 1934, wrote a letter to the Master General of the Dominican Order and stated:

"It may justly be said that the Rosary of Mary is, as it were, the principle and foundation on which the very Order of St. Dominic rests for making perfect the life of its members and obtaining the salvation of others."[15]

St. Catherine of Siena said: "The voice of Dominic's preaching is still heard today and will continue to be heard in the preaching of his followers."

A former Master General of the Dominican Order, the late Anicetus Fernandez, O.P., stated to Dominicans in 1963 at an International Rosary Congress in Rome, the following:

> "Given that the Rosary came to us from the hands of Our Lady herself, a most grave obligation devolves on us. The Popes have given us and no one else the full power and responsibility for bringing it to the people."

At the same Rosary Congress, a former Master General of the Dominican Order, the late Cardinal Michael Browne, O.P., stated: "The future of the Dominican Order and its apostolate rests on its faithfulness in preaching the Rosary." Also, the late Cardinal Luigi Ciappi, O.P., one time papal theologian, stated to Dominicans at the Rosary Congress:

> "Grateful to Divine Providence for having chosen the Dominican Order to spread abroad the Rosary of Mary, let us use the Rosary, in imitation of our Father Dominic, as a very efficacious means of personal sanctification, as a banner of truth and evangelical virtue."

In his apostolic exhortation *Marialis Cultus* (see Appendix 2), Paul VI addressed the Dominican Order as *the guardians and promoters of the Rosary*. Vincent De Couesnougle, O.P., the Master General in the 1970s and 1980s made a statement on January 6, 1975, that was directed to all Dominicans:

> "A tradition recognized in the Church makes us heirs of the mission given to our Father Dominic by the Blessed Virgin: "Go and preach my Rosary." This is a heritage of which we should be proud and from which we should be the first to benefit in our lives and in our prayer."[16]

In an address at the Pontifical University of St. Thomas Aquinas in Rome in 1994, Pope John Paul II stated:

> "The Dominican is called to delve into the mysteries of Christ through prayer, particularly with the Rosary."[17]

It is most fitting to end this chapter with an excerpt from one of Pope Leo XIII's Rosary encyclicals entitled *Supremi Apostulatus*:

"St. Dominic composed the Rosary in such a way that the mysteries of our salvation are recalled to mind in succession. This method of meditation is interspersed and, as it were, interlaced with the Hail Mary and with the prayer of God, the Father of our Lord Jesus Christ. We who are searching for a remedy for similar evils have the right to believe that, by using the same prayer St. Dominic used to accomplish so much good in the Catholic world, we too will see the calamities of our times disappear."[18]

Chapter 3

The Rosary: Mary's School

I n an audience on May 28, 1997, John Paul II stated:

> "In the nascent Church, Mary passed on to the disciples her memories of the Incarnation, the infancy, the hidden life and the mission of her divine Son as a priceless treasure, thus helping to make him known and to strengthen the faith of believers."[1]

In this passage we see Mary as teacher. She is the best of teachers, the one most equipped and qualified for teaching us the mystery of her Son. The Rosary is her school wherein we enroll to learn the mystery of Christ.

In Mary, we have a teacher who is the most perfect example of Christian contemplation. Mary kept all the memories of her Son's life in her heart. St. Luke refers to Mary in his Gospel as a contemplative:

> "But Mary kept all these things, pondering them in her heart (LK 2:19)."

There is some consensus among biblical historians that Luke lived in the company of Mary for some time. Luke received knowledge from Mary concerning Jesus' life. This image of the disciple Luke being a student of Mary takes us back to an audience of John Paul II on May 7, 1997, where he said:

"At the school of the Virgin, the disciples learn to
know the Lord deeply, as John did, and to have an
intimate and lasting relationship with him."[2]

In his Gospel, Luke refers to Mary pondering in her heart, heart
here referring to her memory, reasoning and judgment. St. Luke
used the Hebrew word *dabar* in describing Mary as keeping all these
things in her heart. The French Dominican Rosary scholar, Mark
Tremeau, O.P., mentions in his book *Mystery of the Rosary* that the
word *dabar* refers to bringing together, to join, hence the idea of
comparing. He sees Mary comparing what she saw and heard with
the earlier revelations she had received. Fr. Tremeau, O.P., states:

"This says it all: she saw (the things) and heard (the
words) the two meanings of *dabar*–and she compared
all that with her own experience and with the wonder
of the divine plan."[3]

According to some scholars, the root of the Hebrew verb *dabar*
comes from hâgâh–meaning repeat, to meditate on, take an interest
in. In this attitude of soul, Mary is seen as keeping in step with her
Jewish ancestors that remembered God's marvelous deeds. The
French Dominican Tremeau mentions in his book that Mary engaged
in an activity of soul that was characteristic of all religious Jews: she
remembered and she considered in her heart. Mary had the gift of
contemplation, but she also sought for insight, practicing active prayer.
Contemplation, as an infused gift and grace, and the engagement of
the mind are compatible as we see in the example of Mary.

The French Dominican Tremeau mentions in his book *Mystery of
the Rosary* that Mary's prayer life was nourished by the mysteries
we call joyful, sorrowful and glorious. Her way of prayer was going
over these mysteries in her memory and searching them in her mind.
When we enroll ourselves in Mary's school, we realize that by meditating on the 15 mysteries of the Rosary, we are following Mary's
method of prayer. We are, as John Paul II states in *Mother of the*

Redeemer, "proceeding along the path already trodden by the Virgin Mary."[4]

As every student knows, effort is required or little will be gained; but as students in Mary's school soon find out, the results are more than worth the effort. In the *beginning of Mary's class,* students learn the Our Father and Hail Mary along with the scenes of the mysteries through pondering the Gospel passages that pertain to each mystery. This includes using our imagination and the "reconstruction of places" proposed by St. Ignatius Loyola in his spiritual exercises whereby we picture to ourselves the mystery we are pondering. Paul VI taught not to say the Our Father, Hail Mary and Glory Be in a mechanical and rapid fashion but at a quiet and lingering pace. In the *middle class,* the students learn that the Rosary is a pocket manual of Christian doctrine by studying and pondering over the Gospel passages, one mystery at a time. The Rosary is a compendium of theology: dogmatic, moral and mystical. Paul VI called the Rosary "a Gospel prayer" in his apostolic exhortation *Marialis Cultus,* which is in Appendix II at the end of this book. The *Catechism of the Catholic Church* calls the Rosary the "epitome of the whole Gospel." In the *higher class,* the students learn that the Rosary is a rule of life and its mysteries form their lives. St. Louis de Montfort calls the mysteries "fifteen pictures whose every detail must rule and inspire our lives." Students also learn to exercise and put into practice the virtue that shines forth in each mystery.

Mary is the one who reveals Jesus to us in the Rosary, just as she revealed Him to the shepherds and the three wise men. In the book of Proverbs of the Old Testament, there is reference to Mary: "He who finds me finds life and wins favor with the Lord (Prov. 8:35)." In this light, he who enrolls in Mary's school, the Rosary, will find life. So many people today are thirsting for the Absolute. Perhaps St. Augustine sums it up best in his *Confessions* for the people of our times: "You have made us for Yourself, O Lord, and our hearts are restless till they rest in you."

Mary's school, the Rosary, is a school of moral formation. Praying for the virtues, along with meditation on the mysteries is part of the Rosary. Each of the 15 mysteries gives us images needed to start a movement toward action. The example of virtue in each of the 15 mysteries penetrates the subconscious and acts on our deepest tendencies. Concentration on the high ideals shown in each mystery stimulates virtue. Bossuet writes of this in his *Discourses on the Mysteries:*

> "To counteract the wayward imagination, we must supply it with good images. When our memory is filled with them, it will reproduce only these devout images."[5]

Pope Leo XIII mentioned in one of his 1893 Rosary encyclicals that by meditating on examples of virtues contained in the mysteries of the Rosary, they become fixed in the memory and produce a change for the better in our thoughts and habits.

St. Louis de Montfort in his classic *Secret of the Rosary* mentions that Mary commissioned St. Dominic to teach the mysteries of the Rosary so that people could pattern their lives and actions upon Jesus' virtues. In his book, St. Louis states:

> "For the Holy Rosary teaches people about the virtues of Jesus and Mary and leads them to mental prayer and to imitate Our Lord and Savior Jesus Christ."[6]

The example of Jesus and Mary in the 15 mysteries can attract us to moral virtue and be a powerful factor for moral progress. In his encyclical *Ingruentium Malorum* of 1951, Pius XII stated:

> "Through frequent meditation on the mysteries, the soul inclines to, and grows in, the virtues they contain. It is filled with hope for the everlasting rewards and feels itself prodded gently yet firmly to follow the way of Christ and His Mother."[7]

In Mary's school, the Rosary is seen as a sacramental, one that leads us to the "Sacrament of sacraments," the Eucharist. Vatican Council II stated that the Eucharist is "the source and summit of the Christian life." The Rosary, as a sacramental, prepares the faithful to receive the fruits of the sacraments. The Rosary helps us meditate on the mystery of Christ which the Church proclaims and celebrates in her liturgy. Pope Paul VI taught that the Rosary was an excellent preparation for the Mass. In *Marialis Cultus* (see Appendix II) he stated:

> "The Rosary is a practice of piety which easily harmonizes with the liturgy. Meditation on the mysteries of the Rosary, by familiarizing the hearts and minds of the faithful with the mysteries of the Rosary, can be an excellent preparation for the celebration of these mysteries in the liturgical action. However, it is a mistake to recite the Rosary during the celebration of the liturgy."[8]

Many people are drawn to pray the Rosary before the Blessed Sacrament in the tabernacle, so as to be enlightened and consoled. Jesus says to us:

> "Come to me, all you who labor and are overburdened, and I will give you rest. Shoulder my yoke and learn from me, for I am gentle and humble in heart and you will find rest for your souls (Mt. 11: 28-30)."

In his book *The Riches of the Rosary*, the Irish Dominican Rosary scholar, Gabriel Harty, O.P., states:

> "All the mysteries of his life are focused on and crystallized in the Eucharist, which might be compared to the sun, around which the other heavenly bodies of our universe revolve."[9]

The sacramental of the Rosary leads us to the Eucharist.
John Paul II states: "Mary guides the faithful to the Eucharist."

John Paul II has called for efforts to evangelize and renew the faith of the Christian people in fidelity to the directives of Vatican Council II. On December 10, 2001, at the Jubilee for Catechists, Cardinal Joseph Ratzinger said:

> "Catechists should have an intense prayer life. That is the basis for every successful campaign of evangelization."[10]

The Rosary is a wonderful prayer for this time of the "new evangelization;" seeing that any evangelization process has its basis in the mysteries of Christ in His Incarnation, Redemption and Resurrection. Former Master General of the Dominican Order Vincent de Cousnongle, O.P., stated in 1975:

> "The Rosary can serve as a framework for a real catechesis and primary evangelization."[11] "It is an evangelical prayer, a way of teaching people how to ponder over the scriptures in prayer and faith."[12]

In the 1500s, the Rosary was described as "more a method of preaching than praying."

St. Louis de Montfort used the Rosary during his priestly life as his main instrument for evangelization. He wrote:

> "For myself, I know no better way of establishing the kingdom of God, Eternal Wisdom, than to unite vocal and mental prayer by praying the Rosary and meditating on the 15 mysteries."[13]

The French Dominican Henri Lacordaire, O.P. (1802-1861) was deeply devoted to the Rosary. He was a famous preacher in France. He was continually invited to preach at Notre Dame Cathedral in Paris. He spent 10 years reestablishing the Dominican Order in France. He spoke of the Rosary as "the Gospel on its knees." Of the Rosary, he said:

> "The Rosary is the great book in which priest and

> the man of the world, if they knew how to read it, will learn better than anywhere else, information of life and the science of the saints. For Christians, the first of all books is the Gospel, and the Rosary is the Gospel in brief."[14]

The Dominican Order has used the Rosary as a syllabus for evangelization. The late Cardinal Michael Browne, O.P., one of the intellectual giants behind Vatican II and former Master General of the Dominican Order, considered the Summa Theologica of St. Thomas Aquinas and the Rosary of St. Dominic as the chief means that the Dominicans have for evangelization. It was Leo XIII in 1892 who referred to the teachings of Aquinas and the Rosary as the two means that the Dominicans have to remedy the wrongdoing of the century.

Council Fathers at the Second Vatican Council (1962-1965) intended to reaffirm the value and validity of certain practices and exercises of piety, such as the Rosary, that have been recommended by the Magisterium of the Church. The Rosary as a school of prayer and holiness has been encouraged by Supreme Pontiffs as an effective means of nourishing the life of faith and devotion to Mary that is authentic and vigorous. The Rosary orients Marian prayer to its proper goal: the glorification of Christ. Paul VI stressed in *Marialis Cultus* (see Appendix 2) that the Rosary is a Gospel prayer. He wrote:

> "As a gospel prayer, centered on the mystery of the redemptive Incarnation, the Rosary is therefore a prayer with a clearly Christological orientation (N. 46)."

Many Popes have praised Mary's school, the Rosary, as a spiritual training school, where people whose muscles of the spirit have grown flabby and atrophied, can slowly win back the strength required to come off victorious in the great battle of life. St. Pius X, who was Pope from 1903-1914, championed Mary's Rosary and encouraged people to enroll in her school. The testament which he wanted to leave to the Church, by which he would be remembered was: *to love the Rosary and pray it every day with devotion.* He always taught that the Rosary was most pleasing to Mary and that it was a prayer that was the most beautiful and richest in graces.

Pope Pius XII compared the Rosary to the sling shot of David with which he overcame Goliath. In his encyclical *Ingruentium Malorum*, he wrote:

> "It is not with physical force, not with arms, not with human power, but with the divine help obtained through the Rosary, that the Church and all its members, strong and undaunted like David with his sling, will be able to confront the infernal enemy."

Blessed John XXIII (1881-1963) was a man very devoted to Mary. In his family, the Rosary was recited every evening. As Cardinal Angelo Roncalli, Archbishop of Venice, he started praying the 15 mysteries each day. When he became Pope in 1958 and took the name John XXIII, he continued to pray the 15 mysteries of the Rosary over the course of the day: the joyful in the morning, sorrowful in the afternoon and the glorious at 7:30 p.m. with the papal family: his secretary, the sisters and housekeepers.

In the Rosary, Blessed John XXIII saw a summary of the Gospel, a school in which to form ourselves in virtues. He saw the Rosary as "a prayer of love breathed from the heart." He was not only a devotee but also an apostle of the Rosary. In his apostolate letter *Il Religiosa Convegno* of September 29, 1961, he stated:

> "The Rosary, as an exercise of Christian devotion among the faithful of the Latin rite, comes after the Mass and Breviary for priests and after participation in the sacraments for the laity."[15]

In regards to the Rosary beads, he refers to them in this apostolic

Blessed John XXIII said: "The Rosary is a summary of the Gospel, a school in which to form ourselves in virtues."

letter in the following words:

> "How sweet to see you held in the hands of the
> innocent, the holy priests, the young and the
> elderly...held by countless pious multitudes as an
> emblem and a standard of hope for peace in hearts
> and among the entire human race."[16]

John Paul II sees the Rosary as Mary's school. On October 2,
1988, he stated:

> "To recite the Rosary indeed means to place oneself
> in Mary's school and to learn from her, Christ's Mother
> and disciple, how to live deeply and freely the
> demands of Christian faith."[17]

John Paul II shows Mary as the teacher of Jesus in his apostolic exhortation *Catechesi Tradendae* when he mentions that Jesus was
formed by her in human knowledge of the Scriptures and the history
of God's plan for his people. In his apostolic exhortation on catechesis,
the Pope called Mary "a living catechism" and "the mother and model
of Catechists." In the Rosary, John Paul II invites us to enter into
confidential conversation with Mary, our teacher. He invites us to
open up our hearts to her, to speak to her of our hopes and sorrows.
   John Paul II encourages families to enter into Mary's school. In
Rome, on October 1, 1995, before coming to New York City, he said:

> "Daily recitation of the Rosary in the family was
> once widespread. How worthwhile would such a
> practice be today! Mary's Rosary removes the seeds
> of family breakup; it is the sure bond of communion
> and peace."[18]

On October 7, 1995, while speaking at St. Patrick's Cathedral in New
York, he encouraged the families of the United States to pray the
Rosary. The Pope's encouragement reflected Paul VI's sentiments
about family prayer. Paul VI pointed to the Second Vatican Council

in its call to the family to be the domestic Church. Paul VI taught that there must be an effort to reinstate family prayer if there is to be a restoration of the family as the domestic Church. Paul VI hoped that when the family gathered for prayer, the Rosary would be a frequent and favored manner of praying. When John Paul II visited Central Park in New York on October 7, 1995, he encouraged people to cling to Mary's Rosary and in so doing, they will never wander far from her side.

In his apostolic exhortation *The Role of the Christian Family in the Modern World*, John Paul II explains to parents their responsibility in educating their children in prayer. The Pope recommended the Rosary to be considered as one of the best prayers in common that the Christian family is invited to recite. In regards to parental responsibility, he wrote:

> "Only by praying together with their children can a father and mother penetrate the innermost depths of their children's hearts and leave an impression that the future events in their lives will not be able to efface."[19]

The saints always made Jesus' life their principle object of study, meditating on His virtues, suffering and glory. Many saints have enrolled in Mary's school, the Rosary. St. Louis de Montfort (1673-1716) was one of these marvelous saints. He was known as the "priest with the big Rosary," as he wore a 15 decade Rosary on his belt. He was born in the town of Montfort in western France. He was ordained a priest in 1700 and for sixteen years walked up and down the coast of France preaching missions. He always recommended the Rosary and established the Confraternity of the Rosary in the parishes where he gave parish missions. He was given the title *Apostolic Missionary* by Pope Clement XI. He was among the few priests in the world who had the faculty of being an *Apostolic Missionary*. Pope John Paul II singled him out in his encyclical *Mother of the Redeemer*.

St. Louis de Montfort was a great apostle of the Rosary. His classic Secret of the Rosary *is a highly recommended book on the Rosary.*

St. Louis was a great disciple of St. Dominic in teaching the Rosary. His great love and admiration for St. Dominic and the Rosary led him to become a member of the Third Order of St. Dominic in 1710 in the Dominican Priory of Nantes. He was able to do this since diocesan priests and lay people are permitted to join the Third Order of St. Dominic, which is a branch of the Dominican Order. He wrote to the Master General of the Dominicans in 1712 and asked permission to preach the Rosary wherever God called him and to enroll as many people as he could into the Rosary Confraternity. In 1713, a priest who knew St. Louis in Paris, said:

> "No one was a more faithful disciple of St. Dominic when it came to the devotion to the Rosary. He recommended its practice to everyone."[20]

St. Louis would use fifteen paintings on the mysteries of the Rosary when explaining the mysteries that are called to mind at the beginning of each decade. This great apostle of the Rosary, a true son of St. Dominic, wrote in his classic *Secret of the Rosary*:

> "There is not anything in the world more moving than the wonderful story of the life, death and glory of Our Savior, unfolding before our eyes in the fifteen mysteries."[21]

He continually urged priests to pray the Rosary and to preach it as a means of converting sinners. He encouraged people to pray the whole Rosary everyday, or at least five decades of it. St. Louis used the Rosary to preach the mercy of God and hope for sinners. This was to counteract Jansenism, a heresy which emphasized the justice of God, without mentioning God's mercy.

His book *Secret of the Rosary* is a classic. It is highly recommended for all people who desire to grow in their understanding of the history of the Rosary, its meaning and how to pray it. In his book, St. Louis quotes many reputable authors and draws heavily from the Dominican Antonin Thomas's book *The Mystical Rose Tree*.

The *Secret of the Rosary* has been called one of the greatest, if not the greatest, book ever written on the Rosary.

St. Louis founded the Missionaries of the Company of Mary. He had the members pray the 15 decades of the Rosary everyday and enroll as many people as possible into the Confraternity of the Rosary. He wanted them to be men as he said:

> "Like Dominic of old who will range far and wide,
> with the Holy Gospel issuing from their mouths like
> a bright and burning flame and the Rosary in their
> hands."[22]

St. Francis de Sales (1567-1622) was the Bishop of Geneva. He is a Doctor of the Church and patron saint of writers. He spent one hour every day praying the Rosary. He believed that the Rosary was the best form of prayer when prayed properly. One day he said to St. Vincent de Paul:

> "If I did not have the obligation of the Divine Office,
> I would say no other prayer than the Rosary."[23]

St. Charles Borremeo (1538-1584), Cardinal Archbishop of Milan, received a doctorate degree in civil and canon law at age 21. He became Archbishop of Milan at age 25. He prayed the Rosary everyday. He strongly recommended it to his priests and to men in the seminaries. He once said:

> "I depend on the Rosary almost entirely for the
> conversion and sanctification of my diocese."

St. Alphonsus Liguori (1696-1787) was the Founder of the Redemptorist Order and Doctor of the Church. He was author of the classic *Glories of Mary*. He received a doctorate degree in law from the University of Naples and practiced law before he became a priest. He is patron saint of confessors and moralists. He was very devoted to the Rosary. He taught that Mary revealed the Rosary to St. Dominic. He wrote:

"The Blessed Virgin said to St. Dominic: 'This land
will always be barren until rain falls on it.'"

St. Alphonsus taught that this rain was devotion to the Rosary and
that St. Dominic was called to teach this devotion. St. Alphonsus
also taught that Mary is more pleased with 5 decades said slowly and
devoutly than 15 decades said in a hurry and with little devotion.

St. Bernadette Soubirous (1844-1879), at the age of 14, experienced 18 apparitions of Mary between February 11 and July 16, 1858.
These apparitions took place in Lourdes, France. Six years after the
apparitions, she entered the convent of the Sisters of Notre Dame at
Nevers, France. Bernadette was always praying the Rosary. As a
child or as a teenager, the Rosary was her favorite prayer. She would
one day say: "As a child, the only thing I knew was the Rosary."

When Mary appeared to Bernadette, the Rosary was always hanging on the right arm of Mary, with the chain being yellow and the
beads being large and white. The late French Archbishop of Toulouse,
Gabriel Garrone, once said at an International Rosary Congress:

"Lourdes is the place of the Rosary. Mary teaches
Bernadette to recite the beads. She urges her sweetly,
ave by ave. She accompanies her in silence until the
Gloria, which she says with her."

When Bernadette finished praying the Rosary, Mary would smile at
her. According to St. Bernadette, it seemed all Our Lady did was
smile. This image of Mary smiling at Bernadette after she prayed
the Rosary, brings to mind what John Paul II said in 1987:

"The prayer of the Rosary will bring the world, with
the smile of the Virgin Mother, the tender tones of
God's love."[24]

St. Bernadette always recommended the Rosary to others. She
would say: "You will never say it in vain." As a nun, Bernadette
would encourage the sisters to pray the Rosary while going to sleep.
She would say, "You will be like a little child who falls asleep say-

ing, 'Mama, Mama!'" Throughout her life in the convent, she suffered from chronic asthma and tuberculosis. When she was ill, she would pray the Rosary all day long. She would pass many sleepless nights praying her Rosary. During these years, her fidelity to the Rosary was marvelous.

Mother Bordenave, one of the Superior Generals who knew and loved her best, said: "The Rosary was the prayer she loved above all." The rhythm of the Rosary was the rhythm of her life. If we were to ask Bernadette to teach us to pray, she would take her Rosary and encourage us to pray it well, to realize what it means and to live what we pray.

Blessed Padre Pio (1887-1968) was a Capuchin priest who lived most of his priestly life at the friary of San Giovanni Rotondo in Italy. Pope Paul VI said in 1971:

> "Look what fame he had–But why? Because he said Mass humbly, heard confessions from dawn to dusk and was one who bore the wounds of our Lord. He was a man of prayer and suffering."[25]

Padre Pio had the stigmata, the marks of Jesus' Passion, in his body for many years. John Paul II said in 1999:

> "His stigmata like those of Francis of Assisi were the work and sign of divine mercy, which redeemed the world by the Cross of Jesus Christ."[26]

Padre Pio was a man of deep prayer. He would say: "In books we seek God, in prayer we find him." He would often say: "Pray, hope and don't worry." Except for when offering Mass, he always had the Rosary in his hands. He would pray for each soul's eternal salvation when praying the Rosary. He would often mention that the Rosary is the prayer in which Mary triumphs over everything and everyone. Padre Pio would say: "The Rosary is a weapon in our hands." When he forgot his Rosary, he would ask a brother to go and get his "weapon."

Blessed Padre Pio was called "the living Rosary."
Before his death he said: "Love Our Lady and help others to
love her. Always recite the Rosary."

Padre Pio was called "the living Rosary." One day his superior asked him how many Rosaries he prayed that day. The answer was 34. When asked what inheritance he wished to leave his spiritual children–he said: "The Rosary." Near the end of his life, he didn't talk much. People would ask him for help, but all he would do was to show them the Rosary. It has been said that the day before he died, people asked him: "Say something to us, Father." His response was mentioned by Pope John Paul II the day he beatified Padre Pio on May 2, 1999. The response was:

> "Love Our Lady and help others to love her. Always
> recite the Rosary."[27]

St. Louis de Montfort encouraged the laity to arm themselves with meditation on the 15 mysteries of the Rosary. Two members of the laity, who have been beatified, took his advice and are true examples for us. They are Pier Giorgio Frassati and Bartolo Longo. Blessed Pier Giorgio Frassati (1901-1925) was born in Turin, Italy. He was a young man who strived after physical and spiritual fitness. He was a marvelous, robust athlete whom John Paul II called, in 1984, *model of athletes.* He was an avid skier, swimmer, bicycle and rowing enthusiast. He belonged to the Italian Alpine Club and was an ardent mountain hiker. The majesty of God was nowhere more apparent to him than on the heights of mountains, especially Mt. Blanc, one of his favorites in Italy.

His friends looked to this marvelous athlete as a natural leader. His Catholic faith was strong as he nourished it through prayer. In 1920, he became a night adorer, one who would spend several hours praying in Church during the night adoring the Risen Christ present in the Blessed Sacrament. His passion for sports and the mountains and his attention to society's problems never lessened his relationship with the Triune God.

Pier Giorgio always had a Rosary in his pocket and would pray it walking along. He loved praying the Rosary. He prayed the Rosary three times a day after he became a member of the Third Order of St.

Blessed Pier Giorgio Frassati, whom John Paul II called model of athletes, *loved praying the Rosary. He always encouraged others to pray it.*

Dominic in 1922. He was a true disciple of St. Dominic in encouraging the praying of the Rosary. When he would go hiking in the mountains with his young friends, he would always say: "Let us say the Rosary." Pier was very active in taking courageous stands in public. When he and his friends from the Catholic movement *Catholic Action* would stand up for Catholic social teaching and be attacked for it, he would hold up his Rosary and call on everyone to pray for themselves and those who were attacking them.

He contracted polio at the age of 24. He died with a smile on his face and a Rosary in his hand. John Paul II said of the young Frassati:

> "He left this world rather young, but he made a mark
> upon our entire century, and not only our century."[28]

John Paul II beatified Pier Georgio on May 20, 1990. Before leaving the altar on this occasion, the Pope said to the young who were in attendance in St. Peter's Square:

> "Dear young people, I invite you to imitate the
> example of the newly beatified. You too must find a
> way to devote yourselves often to prayer and
> meditation along with the Mother of the Redeemer in
> order to rejuvenate your faith and to find inspiration
> for your service to Christ and the Church in the life
> example of Mary most holy."[29]

Pier Frassati would surely hold up the Rosary to the young and say: "This is the way!"

Blessed Bartolo Longo (1841-1926) was a 20th century apostle of the Rosary. He received his law degree at age 23 and graduated from the University of Naples in Italy. While studying there he attended seances and gradually was made a priest in a Satanic cult. A Dominican priest, Father Alberto Radente, O.P. helped him withdraw from the Satanic cult and reintroduced him to the Catholic faith. On March 25, 1871, this young lawyer became a member of the Third Order of St. Dominic. This true disciple of St. Dominic was destined to become one of the greatest modern apostles of the Rosary. In prayer to Mary, Bartolo said:

> "I shall not depart this earth without first displaying before you, the triumph of your Rosary."

As a member of the Third Order of St. Dominic, Bartolo wrote:

> "Come, children listen to me, Mary says. Come to the school of my Rosary and I shall teach you holy love and the short and sure way to arrive to heaven."[30]

In 1872, while walking on a road called Arpaia in the Valley of Pompei, he heard a voice in his soul whisper to him:

> "If you wish to be saved, you must spread the Rosary. It is Mary's promise: 'He who spreads the Rosary is saved.'"[31]

Taken by surprise, Bartolo shouted out:

> "If it is true that you promised St. Dominic that he who spreads the Rosary is saved, then I shall not leave this land of Pompei before having spread your Rosary."[32]

Bartolo married Marianna de Fusco in 1885 at the age of 44. He was an avid writer. He said: "O God! In one hand, you placed the Rosary, in the other, a pen." He published a magazine called *Il Rosario E La Nuova Pompei* in 1884 and wrote the book *The Fifteen Saturdays*. Bartolo proved that the Rosary is an effective way of bringing people back to Christ by the contemplation of the mysteries of the Rosary. The local bishop urged him to construct a Rosary chapel, which today has become the great Pontifical Sanctuary of Our Lady of the Rosary of Pompei.

Bartolo knew that the ills of society were caused by the forgetfulness of Christ and that the Rosary was a splendid means of introducing Christ into society. Of the Rosary, he wrote:

Blessed Bartolo Longo, one of the greatest modern apostles of the Rosary, was called "Man of Mary" and "Apostle of the Rosary" by John Paul II.

> "The Rosary is a trilogy; it recalls the joys, sorrows and triumphs of Jesus and in perfect symmetry, for each part, it has five chants, and each chant in turn is an episode. The Rosary could very well be called the poem of human redemption."[33]

Bartolo Longo died on October 5, 1926, at the age of 85. His death was followed by many miracles. He was beatified on October 26, 1980, by John Paul II, who called him the "Man of Mary" and "Apostle of the Rosary". John Paul II said of Blessed Bartolo:

> "With the Rosary in his hand, he says to us: 'Reawaken your trust in the Blessed Virgin of the Rosary. You must have the faith of Job!'"[34]

The Rosary is a marvelous school wherein Mary introduces us to Christ as she did to the shepherds and wise men. This splendid school will ensure that while Mary is honored, her Son will be known, loved and glorified. This wonderful school will be our defense against the errors and deviations that Paul VI brought out in *Marialis Cultus* (see Appendix 2) such as: vain credulity, sterile sentimentality, searching for novelties or extraordinary phenomena. Devotion to the Rosary is intended to glorify God and lead Christians to commit themselves to a life which is in absolute conformity with God's will. In Mary's school, she will be the "Star of the New Evangelization, the radiant dawn and a sure guide for our steps."

Chapter 4

John Paul II: "The Rosary: My Favorite Prayer"

A S A YOUNG MAN of 19 or 20, Karol Wojtyla (John Paul II) belonged to a prayer group called the Living Rosary. It was led by a layman, Jan Tyranowski (1901-47). Tyranowski was a 40-year-old bachelor who lived with his mother and brother in the Debniki quarter of Krakow, Poland. He worked as a tailor using machines left over from his father, also a tailor. He was a great reader and a true contemplative as he spent 4 hours everyday in prayer and meditation. He gave close study to the Carmelites, St. John of the Cross (1542-91), St. Theresa of Avila (1515-82), and St. Thérèse of Lisieux (1873-97), all of whom have been declared Doctors of the Church.

Beginning on March 17, 1940, Jan Tyranowski met with Karol Wojtyla and other members of the Living Rosary on a weekly basis. The Living Rosary consisted of 15 young men who would pray one decade a day, while meditating on a particular mystery of the Rosary. Tyranowski's instructions to the young were adopted to the levels of ability and growth in the spirituality of the Rosary. He would teach them to model their lives on Christ in the light of their temperaments. Perhaps thinking back to his own days in the Living Rosary, John Paul II, on April 25, 1987, said the following to a group of young members of the Living Rosary:

Jan Tyranowski was called "a great apostle of the Living Rosary" by John Paul II in 1996.

> "As you recite your 'mystery' or 'decade', you are
> following the inspiration of the Holy Spirit who, by
> means of interior instruction, is leading you to ever
> closer imitation of Jesus, making you pray with Mary,
> and above all, like Mary."[1]

The Living Rosary would meet on Sunday evenings after adoration of the Blessed Sacrament. The members were given a white card with a text relating to the particular mystery of the Rosary they were to meditate on for one month. Tyranowski would assign them a new mystery on each third Sunday of the month. He taught them that these mysteries were to be embodied in each of their lives. The Living Rosary was originally founded by Pauline Jaricot in Lyons, France in 1826. She formed small groups consisting of 15 persons, each person being obliged to pray one decade a day while meditating on a particular mystery.

It was through prayer to Mary and the exercise of self-discipline that Tyranowski sought the salvation of the young in his Living Rosary groups. John Paul II has mentioned that Tyranowski had influenced his way of praying to Mary. When coming to the Living Rosary, he thought of Mary as guiding us to Christ; but Tyranowski helped him to also see Christ guiding us to his own mother, Mary. It was Jan Tyranowski that suggested to Karol Wojtla to read St. Louis de Montfort's classic *True Devotion to Mary*. His papal motto *Totus Tuus* ("I am completely yours, O Mary") came from the Marian spirituality contained in this book. The Pope has referred to this book as having greatly helped him. He once said:

> "The reading of this book was a decisive turning
> point in my life."[2]

By the year 1945, Tyranowski had formed 6 Living Rosary groups, consisting of 90 young men. Eleven vocations to the priesthood came from the Living Rosary groups. One of the eleven young men who would one day become a priest and also a biographer of the Pope, was Miecgyslaw Malinski. He said of Tyranowski: "His influence with Lolek (John Paul II) was gigantic."

Under Tyranowski, Karol Wojtyla made long intervals of silent prayer and mediation a part of his day. Fr. Alexander Drosd, spiritual director and confessor of Tyranowski wrote to Father Karol Wojtla in 1958 concerning Tyranowski. He wrote:

> "He was certainly a mystic. He was a spiritual Alpinist and had the deepest spirituality he has encountered in 25 years. Grace radiated from his face, his eyes, his person, demanding reverence."

When Cardinal Karol Wojtya became Pope John Paul II, he wrote of Tyranowski: "He was a very important person in my life and in my way to the priesthood. He showed me the beauty of eternal life."

In 1996, John Paul II wrote of Tyranowski: "He was a great apostle of the Living Rosary." Perhaps the Pope thought back to his days in the Living Rosary when he said in 1980:

> "Dear young people, esteem the Rosary, raise a joyful song to the Queen of Heaven, and may you delight in reciting it."[3]

Faithful to Jan Tyranowski's memory, the Pope, when he was a young priest in 1948, started up a Living Rosary group for the young in his first parish assignment, the Church of the Assumption in Niegowic, eighteen miles from Krakow. In 1949, John Paul II as a young priest wrote his first article for the Krakow Catholic weekly paper *Tygodnik Powszechny*. The title of the article was "The Apostle" and it was about Jan Tyranowski. In his book *Crossing the Threshold of Hope*, John Paul II stated:

> "Before entering the seminary, I met a layman named Jan Tyranowski, who was a true mystic. This man, whom I consider a saint, introduced me to the great Spanish mystics and in particular to St. John of the Cross."[4]

Jan Tyranowski, an apostle of the Rosary, died in a Krakow hospital on March 15, 1947. As part of the diocesan process for his beatification, a commission was formed in 1997 to study his life. In March of 1998, his remains were brought from a cemetery in Krakow to St. Stanislaw Kostka Church in Debniki, which was his life long parish.

When John Paul II was a boy growing up in his hometown of Wadowice at the foot of the Beschidi mountains in southern Poland, he and his father would pray the Rosary everyday after the bells rang out sounding the Angelus prayer. They would end the Rosary with the Salve Regina. After he became Pope, John Paul II stated that the Rosary was his "favorite prayer." As a priest and Bishop, he was known to go out regularly to Kalvaria Zebrzydowska, the principle Marian shrine of the Archdiocese of Krakow. There he would walk along the paths through the hills meditating and praying the Rosary. When there was snow or ice on the ground he would be seen with a ski pole in one hand and a Rosary in the other. He and his father would regularly come to Kalvaria, to this beautiful Marian shrine, when he was a boy growing up in Wadowice, a town only 10 miles from Kalvaria. Today, in front of this beautiful shrine, there is a statue of John Paul II holding a Rosary in his hand.

The Pope is a very prayerful person. He believes in handing on to others the fruits of prayer, to communicate to others one's thoughts that are passed through prayer. He sees Marian prayer, such as the Rosary, as an inner pilgrimage; which, with Mary's help, will lead us to the spiritual mountain of holiness. He also sees the Rosary as a sweet chain that joins one to God. According to the Pope, personal holiness is a call for training in holiness. In his 84-page apostolic letter *For the New Millennium* that he signed on January 6, 2001, he states:

> "This training in holiness calls for a Christian life distinguished above all in the art of prayer."[5]

Lord Longford, in his book *John Paul II-An Authorized Biography*, mentions that the Pope writes his encyclicals on his knees. When he

This is a statue of John Paul II holding a Rosary at Kalvaria Zebrzydowska, a Marian shrine in southern Poland.

was the Cardinal Archbishop of Krakow, he would talk to a visitor for awhile and then suggest that they pray the Rosary together.

As a Cardinal, John Paul II was invited to the Vatican by Paul VI to give a Lenten retreat on March 7-13, 1976. The structure of the retreat was based in part on the 5 joyful, 5 sorrowful and 5 glorious mysteries of the Rosary. When Pope, John Paul II went to Poland in 1997 and said:

> "The rhythm of the Rosary measures time in Poland,
> it prevades it and forms it."[6]

It did not take John Paul II long after he was made Pope on October 16, 1978, to disclose his sentiments about the Rosary. At a Vatican address on October 29, 1978, he stated:

> "The Rosary is my favorite prayer. A marvelous prayer! Marvelous in its simplicity and in its depth. It can be said that the Rosary is a prayer-commentary on the last Chapter of the Constitution *"Lumen Gentium"* of Vatican II."[7]

Five months after he said this, he began praying the Rosary on Vatican Radio every First Saturday of the month.

The Pope sees Chapter 8 of *Lumen Gentium* (see Appendix 1) as the Magna Carta of Mariology for our age. This chapter is the most extensive magisterial teaching on Mary in the history of the Catholic Church. The Pope views the Rosary as a prayer commentary on this chapter, which deals with the presence of Mary in the mystery of Christ and the Church. In his book, *Crossing the Threshold of Hope*, He said:

> "When I participated in the Council, I found reflected in this chapter all my earlier youthful experiences, as well as those special bonds which continue to unite me to the Mother of God in ever new ways."[8]

*Shortly after he was made Pope, John Paul II started praying
the Rosary on Vatican Radio every First Saturday.*

After approving *Lumen Gentium*, Paul VI referred to Catholic doctrine on Mary as the key to the exact understanding of the mystery of Christ and the Church.

John Paul II has given many addresses on the Rosary throughout his papacy. He speaks of Leo XIII, who wrote 12 encyclicals on the Rosary, as one who left to those who would succeed him a legacy to promote the Rosary. John Paul II has been faithful to this legacy of Leo XIII to promote the Rosary. He continues to teach: "Make the Rosary the sweet chain that binds you to God; through Mary." The Pope also teaches by example, as when he travels, he is often seen praying with the Rosary in his hands.

The Pope went to Pompei, Italy, to the famous Pontifical Sanctuary of Our Lady of the Rosary of Pompei in October of 1979. This Pontifical Sanctuary was founded by Blessed Bartolo Longo, a lawyer and member of the Third Order of St. Dominic. A picture of the Queen of Holy Rosary was given to him by someone who obtained it in the city of Naples. Bartolo placed the picture on the altar of a little run down church in the Valley of Pompei. Many people came to pray the Rosary before this picture. Miracles started to take place. The church was too small to hold all the people, so Bartolo started asking for donations to construct a Rosary sanctuary. It was built and Bartolo gave it over to the Holy See, thus it became a Pontifical Sanctuary.

Blessed Padre Pio as a boy loved going to the Rosary Sanctuary that Blessed Bartolo built. As a soldier stationed in Naples, Padre Pio frequently visited and prayed there. Pope John Paul II beatified Bartolo Longo on October 26, 1980, and on this occasion called him "the Apostle of the Rosary" and "Man of Mary." The Pope referred to Blessed Bartolo as always being obedient to the Pope and to the Church.

From this famous Rosary Sanctuary, John Paul II spoke of the Rosary as the prayer that Mary prays together with us just as she prayed together with the Apostles in the Upper Room. This is a recurring theme of the Pope when he speaks of the Rosary. He has mentioned this theme on different occasions. On November 3, 1981, he stated:

> "The Rosary is a prayer 'concerning Mary' united
> with Christ in His salvific mission. At the same time
> it is a prayer 'to Mary'-our best mediatrix with her
> Son. It is a prayer that in a special way we recite with
> Mary as the apostles in the Upper Room prayed with
> her preparing themselves to receive the Holy Spirit."[9]

He also brought up another theme at the Rosary Sanctuary; that of
meditating with Mary on the mysteries of the Rosary; which she, as
Mother, pondered in her heart. He has returned to this theme on a
number of occasions. In 1997, he stated:

> "In meditating on the mysteries of the Rosary, we
> see through Mary's eyes the mysteries of the Lord's
> life, his Passion, Death and Resurrection. We relive
> them in her Mother's heart."[10]

In 1987, during the Marian Year, the Pope said:

> "In the Rosary we contemplate the mysteries of
> Christ through the eyes of Mary: it is she who reveals
> them to us, helps us to appreciate them, brings them
> within our grasp–'scales them down' to our littleness
> and weakness."[11]

On May 13, 1981, as the Pope was doing a round in St. Peter's
Square in his white jeep, a firing of four shots rang out at 5:17 p.m.
Three bullets from the gun of Turk, Mehmet Ali Agca, struck him,
one in the abdomen, one in the right arm and one in his left hand. He
fell into the arms of his secretary, Msgr. Stanislaw Dziwisz and was
rushed to the hospital. On his way there, he was heard saying: "Mary,
my Mother! Mary, my Mother!" Upon reaching the hospital, he was
taken immediately in for a 5 hour operation. In 1994, as he was
recovering from a broken hip, he wrote a message to the Italian Bishops regarding this event. He wrote:

> "It was a mother's hand that guided the bullet's path and in his throes the Pope halted at the threshold of death."[12]

After the failed assassination attempt of May 13, 1981, John Paul II went to the Marian shrine of Fatima in Portugal on May 12 and 13, 1982. He offered thanksgiving to Mary for her protection during the attempt made on his life one year earlier, on the feast of Our Lady of Fatima. He arrived on the evening of May 12 at the Chapel of Apparitions at Fatima. The Pope opened a box, drew out a golden Rosary, and entwined it over the hands of the statue of Our Lady of Fatima. He then addressed the people, saying:

> "Do you want me to teach you a 'secret'? It is simple, and it is no longer a secret; pray, pray very much; recite the Rosary everyday."[13]

He then knelt down and with a candle in his left hand and a Rosary in his right hand, started to pray the glorious mysteries. The Pope gave the shrine of Fatima one of the bullets that were fired at him on May 13, 1981. It has been embedded in the crown that adorns the statue of Our Lady of Fatima.

On the next day, May 13, John Paul II met with Sister Lucia and offered her a box of Rosaries. Sister Lucia, a Carmelite nun, is the only one of the three children that is still alive who Mary appeared to at Fatima, Portugal, from May to October 1917. Sister Lucia in return offered John Paul II a box of 100 Rosaries that she had made herself. In his homily at Mass that day, he said:

> "The lady of the message of Fatima indicates the Rosary, which can rightly be defined as 'Mary's prayer,' the prayer in which she feels particularly united with us. The Rosary prayer embraces the problems of the Church, of the See of St. Peter, the problems of the whole world. In it, we also remember sinners, that they may be converted and saved and the

souls in purgatory."[14]

Before leaving Fatima for Rome on May 13, John Paul II went back in the late afternoon to the Chapel of the Apparitions. There he prayed for 45 minutes. He prayed at the exact hour (5:17 p.m.) that he was shot in Rome one year earlier on May 13, 1981. He took his Rosary and sank in deep contemplation.

John Paul II sees the Rosary as a confidential conversation that we have with Mary speaking with confidence about one's sorrows and hopes. In 1988, in St. Peter's Square, the Pope spoke of the Rosary as a confidential conversation and not a matter of repeating formulas. He said:

> "In the reciting of the Rosary, it is an entering into confidential conversation with Mary, of speaking to her, telling her of one's hopes, confiding to her one's sorrows, opening one's heart to her."[15]

John Paul II returned to Portugal in 1991 for a pastoral visit from May 10-13. On May 13, he made a return trip to the shrine of Fatima where he thanked Mary for her motherly protection during the attempt made on his life 10 years earlier on the feast of Our Lady of Fatima. On May 12, John Paul went to Madeira and said this of the Rosary:

> "Fervently pray to Mary Most Holy! Feel that she is at your side and consecrate yourselves to her, renewing your confidence and affection throughout the day so that she may help you in your daily needs. May her memory be alive in families, especially through the daily recitation of the Rosary. It is a daily appointment which you and I do not miss; if you want to be close to the Pope's heart for a few moments, I suggest the time of the Rosary, in which I remember everyone to the Virgin Mary, and I would appreciate it if you would remember me to her in the same way."[16]

On October 26, 1997, Pope John Paul II stated in his Angelus message:

> "Today I would like once again to propose that all Christian families pray the Rosary, so that they may taste the beauty of pausing together to meditate, with Mary, on the joyful, sorrowful and glorious mysteries of our Redemption, and thus to sanctify the joyful and difficult moments of daily life. Praying together helps the family to be more united, peaceful, and faithful to the Gospel. May, Mary, Queen of the Holy Rosary, be every family's teacher and guide in this prayer, which is particularly dear to me."[17]

The Pope sees the Rosary as a spiritual oasis for the individual and for the family where courage and confidence can be daily attained.

In 1998, the Pope again emphasized the value of individuals and families praying the Rosary. He stressed the fact that:

> "The Rosary dispels the seeds of family disintegration and that it is a sure bond of communion and peace."[18]

He referred to the importance of rediscovering the Rosary and appreciating its value, as it once was prayed and appreciated. It was a call to find time for prayer. It recalls what the Pope said in London, England, in 1982:

> "It is Mary who will help us find time for prayer. Through the Rosary, that great Gospel prayer, she will help us to know Christ. We need to live as she did, in the presence of God, raising our minds and hearts to Him in our daily activities and worries."[19]

In October of 1999, John Paul II took another opportunity to speak of the value of the Rosary. He said:

"The Rosary itself is a contemplative prayer and is also a powerful form of intercession: indeed, whoever recites it is united with Mary in meditating on the mysteries of Christ and is led to ask her for the grace of these same mysteries in the various situations of life and history."[20]

The Pope has made mention of the Rosary being prayed in order to safeguard the integrity of the faith and to sustain the Church as she enters the third millennium. He sees the Rosary as helping the Church continue to be a prophetic "sign and instrument . . . of communion with God and of the unity of the whole human race" (*Lumen Gentium*, N.1). The Pope also finds in the Rosary a way of finding the fullness of one's baptismal vocation and the sharing in the prophetic, priestly and kingly mission of Christ.

On October 7, 2000, the feast of Our Lady of the Rosary, the Pope and over 1400 Bishops from every continent of the globe gathered around the statue of Our Lady of Fatima in St. Peter's Square to pray the Rosary. Not since the time of Vatican Council II (1962-1965) has such a large and representative a gathering of the world's Bishops taken place. This statue came from the Portuguese Shrine of Our Lady of Fatima. On the evenings of October 6 and 8, this statue was in the Pope's private chapel. The crown that adorns the statue has embedded in it a bullet that was fired at John Paul II on May 13, 1981. The statue also has hanging from its hands, a chain with a ring that the Pope received from the late Cardinal Wyszynski of Warsaw, Poland. The Pope left this ring at the foot of the statue of Mary when he traveled to the Fatima shrine on May 13, 2000, for the beatification of Jacinta and Francisco, two of the three children that Mary appeared to at Fatima in 1917.

The Pope referred to it being natural to pray the Rosary on October 7, 2000, because this date was also the Jubilee for Bishops, the first Saturday of the month and the feast of Our Lady of the Rosary. The Rosary is a main part of the Fatima message in that Mary asked that it be prayed everyday. On this occasion of praying the Rosary, the Pope said:

> "Our prayer this evening takes place in the light of the message of Fatima, the contents of which aid our reflection on the history of the 20th century."[21]

The leading of the five glorious mysteries of the Rosary was entrusted on October 7 to representatives: a Cardinal, a Bishop and a family-of the five continents: Oceania, Asia, America, Africa and Europe. Sister Lucia and members of her Carmelite Monastery in Portugal participated in the fifth glorious mystery. The Pope mentioned that the praying of the Rosary that night was a preparation for the collegial "Act of Entrustment" to the Immaculate Heart of Mary made the next day, October 8. He referred to the praying together of the Rosary as taking the attitude of the Apostles in the Upper Room, gathered with Mary in unanimous and united prayer. At the end of the Rosary, Vatican ushers carried the statue of Our Lady of Fatima through St. Peter's Square to "Mater Ecclesiae" Monastery where it remained for the night.

On October 8, there was a procession of 1400 Bishops and 76 Cardinals leading up to the Mass they concelebrated with John Paul II. At the end of the Mass, there was a collegial "Act of Entrustment" to the Immaculate Heart of Mary. The Pope entrusted to Mary's maternal care the Bishops, the Church and the entire world. The Pope prayed that Mary would join the Church in praying for a new outpouring of the Holy Spirit as she did with the Apostles at Pentecost.

In John Paul II's apostolic letter *For the New Millennium*, which he signed on January 6, 2001, he wrote:

> "Together, we must all imitate the contemplation of Mary, who returned home to Nazareth from her pilgrimage to the Holy City of Jerusalem treasuring in her heart the mystery of her Son (LK 2:51)."[22]

*John Paul II and many Bishops from all over the world
gathered around the statue of Our Lady of Fatima to pray the
Rosary on October 7, 2000, at St. Peter's Square.*

Vatican ushers carried the statue of Our Lady of Fatima through St. Peter's Square on October 8, 2000.

This imitation of Mary's contemplation brings to mind what John Paul II said in 1983:

> "All of us who love the Angel's salutation strive to 'participate' in the meditation of Mary. We strive to do this above all when we recite the Rosary. In motherly fashion, she presides over our prayer. She brings together all over the earth the immense company of those who, 'in unison with her,' meditate on the mystery of the world's redemption by reciting the Rosary."[23]

On March 11, 2001, at the beatification Mass for 233 martyrs who were persecuted during the Spanish Civil War in the 1930s, John Paul II said:

> "They found constant support in the Holy Rosary, recited alone or in small groups, for facing the supreme moment. How effective is this traditional Marian prayer in its simplicity and depth. The Rosary gives powerful help to countless believers in every age."[24]

John Paul II prays the Rosary at the
Chapel of the Apparitions at Fatima on May 12, 1982.

Chapter 5

The Lady of the Rosary

In 1982, the Vicar of Christ, John Paul II, came to Fatima as a pilgrim. He said:

> "I have come on pilgrimage to Fatima with the Rosary beads in my hand.[1] The Lady of the message points to the Rosary."[2]

The Pope stated that the Rosary can be defined as "Mary's prayer and the prayer in which she feels particularly united to us."[3]

The Lady of the Rosary came to Fatima, Portugal, in 1917. She appeared to three children: Jacinta, age 7, Francisco, her brother, age 9, Lucia, their cousin, age 10. She appeared to them six times from May 13 to October 13. On October 13, she said:

> "I am the Lady of the Rosary. I want a chapel built here in my honor. Continue to pray the Rosary every day."[4]

On each of the six apparitions, Mary's message was clear: "Pray the Rosary every day. The Rosary had been introduced by the Dominicans in Portugal, which is known as the "Land of Mary," during the reign of Sancho II in 1224-1247.

Jacinta, the youngest, was questioned on September 27, 1917, by the Reverend Dr. Manuel Formigao, canon theologian to the Cardinal Patriarch of Lisbon. He asked her what was the chief thing that Our Lady told Lucia. Her prompt reply was: "That we should pray the Rosary every day." A year after the apparitions, in May of 1918, Mary appeared to Jacinta in the parish church of St. Anthony and showed her the tableau of the 15 mysteries of the Rosary, teaching her how to meditate on the mysteries, so as to pray the Rosary "properly." According to the 1989 decree of the Congregation of Causes of Saints, Jacinta venerated Mary with a tender and joyful love, honoring her many times with the praying of the Rosary.

Francisco became a dedicated student in Mary's school, the Rosary, after the apparitions. According to the Congregation for the Causes of Saints, Francisco prayed the 15 decades of the Rosary every day and many more times besides. Mary had told Lucia that Francisco would go to heaven, but first he must pray many Rosaries. In 1918, he became very sick; nevertheless, he prayed many Rosaries (seven or eight a day) and exhorted others to pray with him.

According to Lucia, her mother told the children to take a Rosary with them and to pray it after lunch, when they took out the flock of sheep. During the July 13 apparition, Lucia recommended to Mary many requests of the people who asked for cures, conversions, etc. Mary responded by saying that it was necessary for those people to pray the Rosary in order to obtain the graces requested. Years later, Lucia would become Sister Lucia and state:

> "My impression is that Our Lady wanted to give ordinary people, who might not know how to pray, this simple method of getting closer to God. The prayer of the Rosary, after the Liturgy of the Eucharist, is what most unites us to God."[5]

Dr. Charlos Mendes, who questioned all three children during the apparitions, in a letter of September 1917, stated:

> "The principle thing which emerges, according to my own analysis, is that the Lady wishes the spread of devotion to the Rosary."[6]

Sister Lucia later stated:

> "The Rosary is the prayer which introduces us more
> intimately to the mystery of the Blessed Trinity and
> of the Blessed Eucharist."[7]

The apparitions of Fatima have long received the approval of the Catholic Church. This was done so on October 13, 1930, by the Bishop of Fatima, José Correia da Silva. Popes have shown favor toward Fatima. Pius XII is known as the Pope of Fatima. He said:

> "The time for doubting Fatima is past; it is now time
> for action."[8]

Blessed John XXIII called Fatima "the center of all Christian hopes" and the message of Fatima" the world's greatest hope for peace." Paul VI went on a pilgrimage of prayer to Fatima on May 13, 1967. For that occasion, he wrote an apostolic exhortation *Signum Magnum* (The Great Sign). In it, he invites all Catholics to renew personally their consecration to the Immaculate Heart of Mary.

As a sign of this personal consecration to the Immaculate Heart of Mary, the Church offers her children the sacramental called the Scapular of Our Lady of Mount Carmel. Pope Paul VI made it known in 1965 that among the devotions recommended by the Magisterium of the Church, the Rosary and Scapular are to be greatly esteemed. Sister Lucia has mentioned that on October 13, 1917, during the miracle of the sun, the three children saw the mysteries of the Rosary in tableau form. Mary appeared as Our Lady of Mount Carmel and held out the Scapular to the world. On August 15, 1950, Sister Lucia stated:

> "Mary meant that all Catholics should wear the
> Scapular as part of the Fatima message. The Scapular
> and the Rosary are inseparable."[9]

In his message on March 25, 2001, for the occasion of the 750th anniversary of the Scapular of Our Lady of Mount Carmel, John Paul II stated that the Scapular is a sign of consecration to the Immaculate

Heart of Mary and is a treasure for the Church. In his message, John Paul II wrote of the Scapular nourishing the devotion of believers and making people sensitive to Mary's loving presence in their lives. The Pope described the Scapular as being a sign of Mary's constant protection. John Paul II stated that he constantly experiences Mary's protection and has worn the Scapular for a long time. In his book *The Gift and the Mystery*, John Paul II states:

> "On a hilltop in Wadowice, there was a Carmelite monastery. People from Wadowice would go there in great numbers, and this was reflected in the widespread use of the scapular of Our Lady of Mount Carmel. I, too, received the scapular, I think at the age of 10 and I still wear it."[10]

At the end of his message of March 25, 2001, John Paul II stated:

> "The Scapular becomes a sign of the 'covenant' and reciprocal communion between Mary and the faithful: indeed, it concretely translates the gift of his Mother, which Jesus gave on the Cross to John and, through him to all of us, and the entrustment of the beloved Apostle and of us to her, who became our spiritual Mother."[11]

John Paul II went to Fatima on May 12 and 13, 1982. There at the shrine, he thanked Mary for saving his life a year earlier in St. Peter's Square. On this occasion, he publicly presented his new encyclical *Centesimus Annus*, which provides a pastoral guideline for building the "civilization of love" over the rubble of atheistic Marxism. It was fitting that John Paul II did this at Fatima, since he calls Fatima "Europe's spiritual capital."

The statue of Our Lady of Fatima from the Chapel of the Apparitions, known as the Capelinha in Fatima, was flown to Rome for the March 25, 1984, celebration at St. Peter's Square where John Paul II, in spiritual union with the Bishops of the world, consecrated the world

This is the Carmelite Monastery in John Paul II's hometown of Wadowice, Poland. It is here he would come to pray and at age 10 receive the Scapular of Our Lady of Mt. Carmel.

to the Immaculate Heart of Mary. The Congregation for the Doctrine of the Faith stated in their official document of June 26, 2000, that Sister Lucia personally confirmed that this solemn and universal act of consecration corresponded to what Our Lady wished. Hence any further discussion or request is without basis.

In 1991, John Paul II visited Fatima on May 13 and made an Act of Entrustment to Mary and again thanked her for saving his life. He also thanked her for the changes that occurred in the nations of Central and Eastern Europe with the collapse of Marxism. According to Sister Lucia, these events were the response to the consecration of the world to the Immaculate Heart of Mary, which was made by John Paul II, in spiritual union with the Bishops of the world, on March 25, 1984.

On the occasion of the 80th anniversary of the miraculous "dance of the sun," John Paul II sent a letter on October 1, 1997, to the Bishop of Leiria-Fatima, Serafim de Sousa Ferreira e Silva. In this message, John Paul II exhorted families and ecclesial communities to recite the Rosary daily. He urged Pastors to pray the Rosary and to teach their people how to pray it. He also urged Pastors to help the faithful fulfill their duties of their state of life by helping them to return to the daily recitation of the Rosary, "this sweet conversation of children with the mother."

John Paul II visited Fatima on May 13, 2000, and in the square of Our Lady of the Rosary Basilica, celebrated a solemn Mass for the beatification of Francisco and Jacinta Marto, two shepherd children who witnessed the appearances of Mary in 1917. Francisco died on April 4, 1919, and Jacinta died on February 20, 1919. Both are entombed in side chapels in the Basilica of Our Lady of the Rosary. John Paul II said to the children in attendance at the beatification ceremony:

> "Ask your parents and teachers to enroll you in the 'school' of Our Lady, so that she can teach you to be like the little shepherds, who tried to do whatever she asked them. I tell you that one makes more progress in a short time of submission and dependence on Mary

than during entire years of personal initiatives, relying on oneself alone. This was how the little shepherds became saints so quickly."[12]

At the end of the beatification Mass on May 13, 2000, Cardinal Angelo Sodano, Secretary of State, announced that the Pope had decided to make public the third part of the "secret" of Fatima. Cardinal Sodano referred to the third part of the "secret" in the following manner:

"The vision of Fatima concerns above all the war waged by atheist systems against the Church and Christians, and it describes the immense suffering endured by the witnesses to the faith in the last century of the second millennium. It is an interminable Way of the Cross led by the Popes of the 20th century."[13]

Cardinal Sodano stated that the vision of the "Bishop clothed in white who prays for all the faithful," that is contained in the third part, is Pope John Paul II. The Cardinal stated:

"As he makes his way with great effort towards the Cross amid the corpses of those who were martyred (Bishops, priests, men and women religious and many lay persons), he too falls to the ground, apparently dead under a burst of gunfire."[14]

Cardinal Sodano mentioned that after the assassination attempt of May 13, 1981, it was clear to John Paul II that it was:

"a motherly hand which guided the bullet's path, enabling the dying Pope to halt at the threshold of death."[15]

Cardinal Ratzinger, in his theological commentary on the "secret" of Fatima, stated:

"That here 'a mother's hand' had deflected the fateful bullet only shows once more that there is no immutable destiny, that faith and prayer are forces which can influence history and that in the end, prayer is more powerful than bullets and faith more powerful than armies."[16]

The Congregation for the Doctrine of the Faith in their document of June 26, 2000, stated that "Fatima is undoubtedly the most prophetic of modern apparitions."[17] In their document, the Congregation states that the first part of the "secret of Fatima" refers to the frightening vision of hell that Mary showed the children. Mary said to the children:

> "You have seen hell where the souls of poor sinners go. To save them, God wishes to establish in the world *devotion to my Immaculate Heart.* If what I say to you is done, many souls will be saved and there will be peace."[18]

The devotion to the Immaculate Heart of Mary as requested by Our Lady of Fatima consists of:

1. On the First Saturday of the month, we are to receive Holy Communion with the intention of making reparation for the insults, sacrileges and indifferences committed against the Immaculate Heart of Mary.
2. Go to Confession on the First Saturday of the month (it can be 8 days before or after) with the intention of making reparation for the insults, sacrileges and indifferences committed against the Immaculate Heart of Mary.
3. Recite the 5 decades of the Rosary on the First Saturday in reparation for the insults, sacrileges and indifferences committed against the Immaculate Heart of Mary.
4. Keep Mary company on the First Saturday for 15 minutes, meditating on the mysteries of the Rosary with her, with the intention of making reparation for the insults, sacrileges and indifferences committed against the Immaculate Heart of Mary.

Mary promised those who practice the First Saturday devotion for five consecutive months will be assisted by her in the hour of death with all the graces necessary for salvation.

Cardinal Joseph Ratzinger, Prefect of the Congregation for the Doctrine of the Faith in Rome, stated in his theological commentary on the "secret" of Fatima the following:

> "The children were given a vision of hell. They saw the fall of 'the souls of poor sinners.' They are told why they have been exposed to this moment: in order to save souls. To reach this goal, the way indicated is *devotion to the Immaculate Heart of Mary*."[19]

Cardinal Ratzinger also noted in his commentary:

> "'The immaculate heart' is a heart which, with God's grace, has come to perfect interior unity and therefore 'sees God.' To be devoted to the Immaculate Heart of Mary means therefore to embrace this attitude of heart, which makes the fiat– 'your will be done'–the defining center of one's whole life."[20]

In regards to the first and second part of the "secret of Fatima", Cardinal Ratzinger states that the phrase 'to save souls' has emerged as the key words.

In regards to the third part of the "secret," Cardinal Ratzinger sees this vision as:

> "The Church's path is thus described as a Via Crusis, as a journey through a time of violence, destruction and persecution. The history of an entire century can be seen represented in this image."[21]

According to Cardinal Ratzinger, the key words for this third part of the "secret of Fatima" is the threefold cry: Penance! Pen-

John Paul II prays before the statue of
Our Lady of Fatima in St. Peter's Square on October 7, 2000.

The statue of Our Lady of Fatima was placed near the main altar in St. Peter's Basilica for the occasion of the Jubilee of Bishops in October of 2000.

ance! Penance! The Cardinal thinks that to understand the "signs of the time" means to accept the urgency of penance, conversion and faith.

Cardinal Ratzinger sees the vision of the third part of the "secret" as concluding with an image of hope. It is an exhortation to prayer as the path of "salvation for souls" and the summons to do penance and come to conversion. Cardinal Ratzinger commented on what Mary's statement: "my Immaculate Heart will triumph" in the "secret" means. He wrote:

> "The heart open to God, purified by contemplation of God, is stronger than guns and weapons of every kind. The fiat of Mary, the word of her heart, has changed the history of the world because it brought the Savior into the world–because thanks to her Yes, God could become man in our world and remain so for all time.
>
> "In the world you will have tribulation, but take heart; I have overcome the world" (Jn 16:33). The message of Fatima invites us to trust in this promise."[22]

It is interesting to note that in John Paul II's book *Crossing the Threshold of Hope*, he states:

> "On this universal level, if victory comes it will be brought by Mary. Christ will conquer through her, because He wants the Church's victories now and in the future to be linked to her."[23]

On the First Saturday of the month, October 7, 2000, John Paul II and around 1500 Bishops assembled in St. Peter's Square for the praying of the glorious mysteries of the Rosary. It was led by John Paul II. This was done in the presence of the statue of Our Lady of Fatima, which was brought from the Fatima shrine at the request of the Pope. On October 8, at the end of the Mass,

John Paul II and the Bishops made an "Act of Entrustment" to the Immaculate Heart of Mary, entrusting the third millennium to Mary.

Chapter 6

The Rosary as a Meditative Prayer

The late Dominican Reginald Garrigou-Lagrange, a teacher of Pope John Paul II when he was a student at the Angelicum in Rome, stated in his splendid book, *Mother of the Savior*:

> "Our Blessed Lady made known to St. Dominic a kind of preaching till then unknown, which she said would be one of the most powerful weapons against future errors and in future difficulties."[1]

When St. Dominic preached the Rosary, he would explain to people all the wonderful insights to be found in each mystery. The mysteries are like windows that we use to look into the world of God.

Pere Mortier in his classic work *The Lives of the Masters General of the Order of Preachers* mentions that St. Dominic used the Rosary as a method of preaching, placing the mysteries, one by one, before the people and in order to draw down the Divine blessing, invited them to pray the Our Father and Hail Mary. Pere Mortier states in his book:

> "From the lips of Dominic, this method of preaching passed to those of his sons. Through the Rosary, St. Dominic remains for ever the great Preacher to wise and ignorant alike."[2]

106

One of Dominic's spiritual sons, St. Louis De Montfort, stated:

> "The Rosary without meditation on the sacred
> mysteries of our salvation would almost be like a body
> without a soul; excellent matter, but without form
> which sets it apart from other devotions."[3]

According to St. Louis De Montfort, meditation on the mysteries of the Rosary brings about marvelous results:

1) it gradually gives us a perfect knowledge of Jesus Christ
2) it purifies our souls, washing away sin
3) it gives us victory over our enemies
4) it makes it easy for us to practice virtue
5) it sets us on fire with love of Jesus
6) it enriches us with graces and merits.

St. Louis taught that meditation on the mysteries of Christ's life and virtues was the means of gaining the perfect knowledge in which eternal life consists. It is like an apprenticeship in preparing for eternal life. Jesus addressed His Father in these words:

> "And eternal life is this: to know You, the only true
> God, and Jesus Christ, whom you have sent" (Jn 17:3).

The Popes have promoted the Rosary as a meditative prayer down through the centuries. Pope St. Pius V, in 1569, speaking of the Rosary said:

> "Once this method of praying became known, the
> faithful began to be enlightened as a result of their
> meditations, and enkindled by these prayers, they
> suddenly became different men. The darkness of
> heresy was dispelled, and the light of Catholic faith
> shone brightly."[4]

St. Pius V in this statement, teaches that meditation is simply thinking and loving. Thought of the mystery comes first and from the thought comes the fire. Meditation enlightens the mind and the spark from the enlightened mind sets the heart on fire.

In his encyclical letter of March 6, 1934, Pius XI stated:

> "Where does the efficacy and power of praying the Rosary come from? Certainly from the very mysteries of the Divine Redeemer which we contemplate and piously meditate."[5]

In the joyful mysteries, we meditate on the wonders of the Incarnation and this nourishes *faith*. Pius XI stated:

> "Above all, the Rosary nourishes the Catholic faith, which grows stronger by meditation on the sacred mysteries and elevates the mind to truths revealed by God."[6]

In the sorrowful mysteries, we meditate on the sufferings and death of Jesus, the price of our Redemption and this stirs up our *love for Jesus*. Pius XI stated:

> "How could love not be made more fervent by the Rosary? We meditate on the suffering and death of our Redeemer and the sorrows of His afflicted Mother. Will we not make a return of love for the love received."[7]

In the glorious mysteries, we meditate on the promise of *future glory* and *resurrection* merited for us by Jesus. Pius XI stated:

> "The Rosary enlivens hope for the things above that endure forever. As we meditate on the glory of Jesus Christ and His Mother, we see heaven opened, and are heartened in our striving to gain the eternal home."[8]

Blessed John XXIII, who convened the Second Vatican Council in 1962, highly recommended the Rosary and emphasized meditation on the mysteries of the Rosary. In his teachings on the Rosary, he helped people to meditate on its sacred mysteries. He taught that the true substance of a well-meditated Rosary consisted in that threefold element: *mystical contemplation, intimate reflection* and *pious intention*. By *mystical contemplation*, he meant the contemplation of each mystery and the truths of the faith that are contained in each mystery which speak to us of the redemption mission of Jesus. By *intimate reflection*, he referred to each person seeing in each mystery the timely and good teaching as it concerns them, their own sanctification and the particular circumstances of their lives. By *pious intention*, he meant the singling out and praying for persons, institutions or needs of a personal or social order.

Pope Paul VI, who presided over the sessions and conclusion of Vatican II, in his apostolic exhortation *Marialis Cultus* (see Appendix 2), wrote of the Rosary:

> "Without the element of contemplation, the Rosary is a body without a soul, and its recitation is in danger of becoming a mechanical repetition of formulas and of going counter to the warning of Christ: 'And in praying do not heap up empty phrases as the Gentiles do; for they think that they will be heard for their many words' (Mt. 6:7). By its nature, the recitation of the Rosary calls for a quiet rhythm and a lingering pace, helping the individual to meditate on the mysteries of the Lord's life as seen through the eyes of her, who was closest to the Lord. In this way the unfathomable riches of these mysteries are unfolded.
>
> ....The Rosary of the Blessed Virgin Mary, according to the tradition accepted by our predecessor, St. Pius V, authoritatively taught by him, consists of various elements disposed in an organic fashion: contemplation in communion with Mary, of a series of mysteries of salvation, wisely distributed into three cycles, these mysteries express the joy of the messianic times, the salvific suffering of Christ and the glory of

the risen Lord which fills the Church. This contemplation by its very nature encourages practical reflection and provides stimulating norms for living."[9]

The Catechism of the Catholic Church, which devotes a section on the mysteries of Christ's life, comments on meditation in the following way:

> "Meditation engages thought, imagination, emotion and desire. This mobilization of faculties is necessary in order to deepen our conviction of faith, prompt the conversion of our heart, and strengthen our will to follow Christ. Christian prayer tries above all to meditate on the mysteries of Christ, as in *lectio divino* or the Rosary."[10]

The whole essence of the Rosary is quiet thinking of the heart. It was the prophet Jeremiah who said: "With desolation is the whole land made desolate, because there is no one who thinks in the heart" (Jeremiah 12:11). It is important to realize that when we meditate on the mysteries of the Rosary, we follow the method of prayer that Mary practiced. Mary meditated on the mysteries that are called *joyful,* she pondered over and considered them continually during the hidden life of Jesus. In the later stages of life, she considered and pondered over the mysteries of Jesus that we meditate on in the *sorrowful* and *glorious* mysteries of the Rosary.

To help us ponder with Mary the fifteen mysteries of the Rosary and experience the Rosary as a meditative prayer, this book makes use of Sacred Scripture passages of the New Testament that pertain to these mysteries. It also uses the writing of St. Thomas Aquinas that pertain to the consideration of each mystery and the virtue to be prayed for. Pope Leo XIII said this of St. Thomas:

> "He may be compared to the sun, for he warmed the world with the warmth of his virtues and filled it with the radiance of his teachings."[11]

Pope Leo XIII said of St. Thomas Aquinas: "He may be compared to the sun, for he warmed the world with the warmth of his virtues and filled it with the radiance of his teachings."

St. Thomas Aquinas (1224-1274) was born in Roccasecca, Italy. He was a spiritual son of St. Dominic and a Dominican teacher par excellence. He is a Doctor of the Church and the Patron of all Catholic schools and has been referred to by many Popes as the "Common Doctor." He studied under St. Albert the Great and received his doctorate degree in Paris.

St. Thomas Aquinas wrote a theological masterpiece called the *Summa Theologica*, a marvelous summary of Catholic theology. The Catholic Church has made his teaching her own. A favorite Thomistic axiom is: "It is better to enlighten than merely to shine; better to give to others the fruits of contemplation than merely to contemplate." St. Thomas was asked where he acquired his knowledge. He pointed to a crucifix on the wall and said: "There is my only book." His sister asked him how to become a saint. He replied: "Will it." In the *Dialogue* of St. Catherine of Siena, God revealed to her the following concerning St. Thomas:

> "Consider the glorious Thomas. With his mind's eye he contemplated my Truth ever so tenderly. He learned more through prayer than through human study. He was a blazing torch shedding light in the Church."[12]

In honor of the seventh centenary of the death of St. Thomas in 1974, Paul VI honored him by going to the Abbey of Fossonova in Italy where Thomas died on March 7, 1274. He also visited Roccasecca, his birthplace and Aquina, the city that gives St. Thomas his name. Paul VI wrote a Letter *"Lumen Ecclesiae"* for this seventh centenary. In it, he wrote:

> "In philosophical and theological studies, he is a guide whom none can replace. Go to Thomas; seek out and read the works of St. Thomas."[13]

Pope John Paul II has given St. Thomas the title "Doctor of Humanity."

It is also hoped that the teachings of Vatican II, the Catechism of the Catholic Church and Pope John Paul II which appear in the following chapters will help us in our meditations and enrich our faith. It is hoped that these meditations will illumine us in pondering, with Mary, the great mysteries of our faith. St. Thomas teaches us that the name "Mary" means "in herself enlightened", and that she will illumine others throughout the world, for this reason she is compared to the sun and to the moon.

It is true that not many people have access to the full five volumes of St. Thomas's *Summa* with its 512 questions, 2,669 articles and 10,000 objections with their solutions. But the Rosary is within the reach of all and can be treasured with its 15 mysteries as our "*Little Summa*". May the Holy Spirit, through Mary and the Rosary, lead us in the third millennium.

Chapter 7

How to Pray the Rosary

Chapter 8 of *Lumen Gentium* states: "Joined to Christ the head and in unity of fellowship with all his saints, the faithful must in the first place reverence the memory of the glorious ever Virgin Mary, Mother of our God and Lord Jesus Christ" (N. 52).

1. Before praying the Rosary, it is helpful to ask Mary to implore the Holy Spirit to pray in you and to help you pray as you ought. It is also good to ask Mary to help you ponder with her while meditating on the mysteries of the Rosary.

2. Meditate on each mystery of the Rosary before you pray the Our Father and Hail Mary. The Gospel passages, such as ones in this book, that center on each mystery are most helpful for each meditation.

3. Ask of God, through the intercession of Mary, for the virtue that shines forth in each mystery, such as the ones in this book, or one of which you are in particular need of.

4. In praying the Our Father and Hail Mary, do so with reverence, tempering the speed which comes all too easily to us. It is helpful to pause briefly several times as you say these two prayers. Pope Paul VI recommended a quiet rhythm and a lingering pace. The Dominican St. Albert the Great advised people to salute Mary in the same way that you would like her to salute you. Chapter 23 comments on the Our Father and Hail Mary.

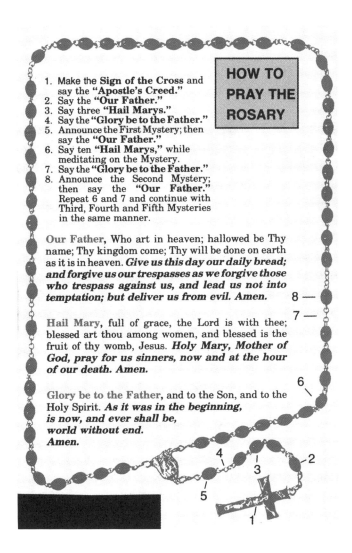

1. Make the **Sign of the Cross** and say the **"Apostle's Creed."**
2. Say the **"Our Father."**
3. Say three **"Hail Marys."**
4. Say the **"Glory be to the Father."**
5. Announce the First Mystery; then say the **"Our Father."**
6. Say ten **"Hail Marys,"** while meditating on the Mystery.
7. Say the **"Glory be to the Father."**
8. Announce the Second Mystery; then say the **"Our Father."** Repeat 6 and 7 and continue with Third, Fourth and Fifth Mysteries in the same manner.

HOW TO PRAY THE ROSARY

Our Father, Who art in heaven; hallowed be Thy name; Thy kingdom come; Thy will be done on earth as it is in heaven. *Give us this day our daily bread; and forgive us our trespasses as we forgive those who trespass against us, and lead us not into temptation; but deliver us from evil. Amen.*

Hail Mary, full of grace, the Lord is with thee; blessed art thou among women, and blessed is the fruit of thy womb, Jesus. *Holy Mary, Mother of God, pray for us sinners, now and at the hour of our death. Amen.*

Glory be to the Father, and to the Son, and to the Holy Spirit. *As it was in the beginning, is now, and ever shall be, world without end. Amen.*

-After each decade say the following prayer requested by the Blessed Virgin Mary at Fatima: "O my Jesus, forgive us our sins, save us from the fires of hell, lead all souls to heaven, especially those who have most need of your mercy."

-Say the "**Hail, Holy Queen**" after the five decades are completed.

-As a general rule, the Joyful Mysteries are said on Monday and Thursday; the Sorrowful Mysteries on Tuesday and Friday; the Glorious Mysteries on Wednesday and Saturday. Depending on the Season, each of the Mysteries is recommended for Sunday.

Promises of Our Lady to those who Devoutly Pray the Rosary

1. Whoever shall faithfully serve me by the recitation of the Rosary, shall receive signal graces.

2. I promise my special protection and the greatest graces to all those who shall recite the Rosary.

3. The Rosary shall be a powerful armour against hell, it will destroy vice, decrease sin, and defeat heresies.

4. It will cause virtue and good works to flourish; it will obtain for souls the abundant mercy of God; it will withdraw the hearts of men from the love of the world and its vanities, and will lift them to the desire of eternal things. Oh, that souls would sanctify themselves by this means.

5. The soul which recommends itself to me by the recitation of the Rosary, shall not perish.

6. Whoever shall recite the Rosary devoutly, applying himself to the consideration of its sacred mysteries shall never be conquered by misfortune. God will not chastise him in His justice, he shall not perish by an unprovided death; if he be just he shall remain in the grace of God, and become worthy of eternal life.

7. Whoever shall have a true devotion for the Rosary shall not die without the sacraments of the Church.

8. Those who are faithful to recite the Rosary shall have during their life and at their death the light of God and the plenitude of His graces; at the moment of death they shall participate in the merits of the saints in paradise.

9. I will deliver very promptly from purgatory those who have been devoted to the Rosary.

10. The faithful children of the Rosary shall merit a high degree of glory in heaven.

11. You shall obtain all you ask of me by the recitation of the Rosary.

12. All those who propagate the Holy Rosary shall be aided by me in their necessities.

13. I have obtained from my Divine Son that all the advocates of the Rosary shall have for intercessors the entire celestial court during their life and at the hour of their death.

14. All who recite the Rosary are all my beloved children, the brothers and sisters of Jesus Christ.

15. Devotion to my Rosary is a great sign of predestination. (Given to St. Dominic and Alan de la Roche, O.P.)

Prayers of the Rosary

The Sign of the Cross --

In the name of the Father, and of the Son, and of the Holy Spirit. *Amen.*

The Apostles' Creed --

I believe in God, the Father Almighty, Creator of Heaven and earth; and in Jesus Christ, his only Son, Our Lord, who was conceived by the Holy Spirit, born of the Virgin Mary, suffered under Pontius Pilate, was crucified, died, and was buried. He descended into hell; the third day he rose again from the dead. He ascended into Heaven, and is seated at the right hand of God, the Father Almighty. From thence he shall come to judge the living and the dead.

I believe in the Holy Spirit, the Holy Catholic Church, the Communion of Saints, the forgiveness of sins, the resurrection of the body, and life everlasting. *Amen.*

Our Father --

Our Father who art in Heaven, hallowed be thy Name. Thy Kingdom come, thy will be done on earth as it is in Heaven. Give us this day our daily bread, and forgive us our trespasses, as we forgive those who trespass against us, and lead us not into temptation, but deliver us from evil. *Amen.*

Hail Mary --

Hail Mary, full of grace, the Lord is with thee; blessed art thou among women, and blessed is the fruit of thy womb, Jesus. Holy Mary, Mother of God, pray for us sinners, now and at the hour of our death. *Amen.*

Glory be to the Father --

Glory be to the Father, and to the Son, and to the Holy Spirit. As it was in the beginning, is now, and ever shall be, world without end. *Amen.*

Hail, Holy Queen --

Hail, Holy Queen, Mother of Mercy, our life, our sweetness, and our hope! To thee do we cry, poor banished children of Eve! To thee do we send up our sighs, mourning and weeping in this valley of tears. Turn then, most gracious advocate, thine eyes of mercy towards us; and after this, our exile, show unto us the blessed fruit of thy womb, Jesus! O clement, O loving, O sweet Virgin Mary!

Pray for us, O holy Mother of God. That we may be made worthy of the promises of Christ.

15 Mysteries of the Rosary

<u>Joyful Mysteries:</u>

    1. The Annunciation
    2. The Visitation
    3. The Birth of Jesus
    4. The Presentation of Jesus in the Temple
    5. The Finding of the Child Jesus in the Temple

<u>Sorrowful Mysteries:</u>

    1. The Agony in the Garden
    2. The Scourging at the Pillar
    3. The Crowning with Thorns
    4. The Carrying of the Cross
    5. The Crucifixion

<u>Glorious Mysteries:</u>

    1. The Resurrection of Jesus
    2. The Ascension of Jesus into Heaven
    3. The Descent of the Holy Spirit
    4. The Assumption of Mary into Heaven
    5. The Coronation of Mary

Chapter 8

<u>**Joyful Mysteries**</u>

1. The Annunciation

According to the Gospel of St. Luke
(Chp. 1:26-35)

IN THE SIXTH month the angel Gabriel was sent from God to a city of Galilee named Nazareth, to a virgin betrothed to a man whose name was Joseph, of the house of David; and the virgin's name was Mary. And he came to her and said, "Hail, full of grace, the Lord is with you!" But she was greatly troubled at the saying, and considered in her mind what sort of greeting this might be. And the angel said to her, "Do not be afraid, Mary, for you have found favour with God. And behold you will conceive in your womb and bear a son, and you shall call his name Jesus. He will be great, and will be called the Son of the Most High; and the Lord God will give to him the throne of his father David, and he will reign over the house of Jacob for ever; and of his kingdom there will be no end."

And Mary said to the angel, "How can this be, since I have no husband?" And the angel said to her, "The Holy Spirit will come upon you, and the power of the Most High will overshadow you; therefore the child to be born will be called holy, the Son of God. And behold, your kinswoman Elizabeth in her old age has also conceived a son; and this is the sixth month with her who was called

John Paul II prays at the Grotto of the Annunciation on March 25, 2000. The Latin inscription under the altar reads: "The Word was made flesh-here" (John 1: 14).

barren. For with God nothing will be impossible." And Mary said, "Behold, I am the handmaid of the Lord; let it be to me according to your word." And the angel departed from her.

Consideration of the Annunciation

"1. It was suitable that it should be made known to the Blessed Virgin that she would conceive Christ.

First of all, that a becoming order of the union of the Son of God with the Virgin might be maintained. Thus St. Augustine says: 'Mary is more blessed in receiving the faith of Christ than in receiving the flesh of Christ. Her nearness as a mother would have been of no profit to Mary had she not borne Christ in her heart after a more blessed manner than in her flesh.'

Secondly, that she might be a more certain witness of this mystery being instructed therein by God.

Thirdly, that she might offer to God the free gift of her obedience which she proved herself ready to do saying: 'Behold the handmaid of the Lord.'

Fourthly, to show that there is a certain spiritual wedlock between the Son of God and human nature. Wherefore, in the Annunciation, the Virgin's consent was asked in place of all human nature. Moreover, the Blessed Virgin did believe explicitly in the future Incarnation, but being humble she did not think such high things of herself.

2. The Annunciation was perfected by the Angel in a suitable order. For the Angel intended three things concerning the Virgin.

First, to render her mind attentive to the consideration of so great an event. This the Angel accomplished by saluting her in a new and unusual salutation. The Angel desiring to render the mind of the Virgin attentive to the announcement of so great a mystery began with her praises: 'Hail, full of grace,' in which salutation he announced her worthiness to conceive, from the fact that she was full of grace, and he proclaimed the conception when he said: 'The Lord is with thee,' and he foretold her consequent honor when he said, 'Blessed art thou among women.'

Secondly, the Angel intended to instruct her concerning the mystery of the Incarnation which was to be fulfilled in her. He did this by announcing that she would conceive and bring forth a Son, and the Angel revealed the dignity of the conceived offspring when he said, "he shall be great and shall be called the Son of the Most High," and likewise the Angel revealed the mode of the conception, when he said, "The Holy Spirit shall come upon thee and the power of the Most High shall overshadow thee."

Thirdly, the Angel intended to induce her mind to consent, which indeed he did through the example of Elizabeth and by reason aided with divine power."[1]

Virtue to be Prayed For - - Faith

"Faith accomplishes four things:

1. By faith the soul is united to God, for through faith the soul enters into a certain union or marriage with God. Baptism is the first sacrament of faith. Therefore the Lord said, 'He who believes and is baptized, shall be saved.'

2. Through faith, eternal life is begun in us, for eternal life is nothing more than to know God. Hence the Lord said, 'This is eternal life that they might know Thee the only true God.' Therefore, it is written, 'Faith is the substance of things to be hoped for' (Heb. 11:1). Therefore, no one can obtain eternal blessedness, which is the true knowledge of God, unless through faith here he first acknowledges God.

3. Faith directs our present life. In order that man might live well, he should know what is necessary to live well. But faith teaches these things; for it teaches there is One God, the Rewarder of the good and the Punisher of the wicked; and that there is another life beyond the grave, and by the knowledge of these things we love good and hate evil.

Faith is that supernatural virtue by which we conquer temptations. This is clear because every temptation is either from the devil, the world, or the flesh. The devil tempts us so that we might not obey God nor subject ourselves to Him. This diabolical temptation is removed through faith, for through faith we know that God is the Lord of all and consequently we are obliged to obey Him.   T h e world tempts us, either by seducing us with its vanities or by terrifying us with its misfortunes. But even these we can conquer through faith, which enables us to believe better things are awaiting us. Hence by faith, we conquer the vanities of this world and fear not its adversities. 'This is the victory which overcometh the world, your faith' (1 Jn. 5:4).

The flesh tempts us by attracting us to the pleasures of the present life, which pleasures at most, are fast, fleeting and perishable. But faith warns us that through these pleasures, if we cling to them improperly, we will lose eternal happiness."[2]

Teachings of Vatican II

"Thus Mary, daughter of Adam, consenting to the Divine Word, became the Mother of Jesus, the one and only Mediator. St. Irenaeus says, she 'being obedient, became the cause of salvation for herself and for the whole human race.' Hence, not a few of the early Fathers gladly assert in their preaching: the knot of Eve's disobedience was untied by Mary's obedience; what the virgin Eve bound through her unbelief, the Virgin Mary loosened by her faith."[3]

"The obedience of faith" is to be given to God who reveals, an obedience by which man commits his whole self to God, offering "the full submission of his intellect and will to God who reveals."[4]

Catechism of the Catholic Church

"The Annunciation to Mary inaugurates "the fullness of time,"[119] the time of the fulfillment of God's promises and preparations. Mary was invited to conceive him in whom the "whole fullness of deity" would dwell bodily"[120] (No. 484).

Chapter 9

2. The Visitation

According to the Gospel of St. Luke
(Chp. 1:39-56)

IN THOSE DAYS Mary arose and went with haste into the hill country, to a city of Judah, and she entered the house of Zechariah and greeted Elizabeth. And when Elizabeth heard the greeting of Mary, the babe leaped in her womb; and Elizabeth was filled with the Holy Spirit and she exclaimed with a loud cry, "Blessed are you among women, and blessed is the fruit of your womb! And why is this granted me, that the mother of my Lord should come to me? For behold, when the voice of your greeting came to my ears, the babe in my womb leaped for joy. And blessed is she who believed that there would be a fulfillment of what was spoken to her from the Lord."

And Mary said, "My soul magnifies the Lord, and my spirit rejoices in God my Savior, for he has regarded the low estate of his handmaiden. For behold, henceforth all generations will call me blessed; for he who is mighty has done great things for me, and holy is his name. And his mercy is on those who fear him from generation to generation. He has shown strength with his arm, he has scattered the proud in the imagination of their hearts, he has put down the mighty from their thrones, and exalted those of low degree; he has filled the hungry with good things, and the rich he has sent empty away. He has helped his servant Israel, in remembrance of his mercy, as he spoke to our fathers, to Abraham and to his posterity for ever." And Mary remained with her about three months and returned to her home.

Consideration of the Visitation

"The Blessed Virgin after conceiving Christ did three things, by which three things are mystically understood what every soul should do after a spiritual conception of the word of God. She hastened to the mountain, saluted Elizabeth, and magnified the Lord. By hastening to the mountain is meant the perfection of virtues; in saluting Elizabeth, fraternal love is shown; while in magnifying the Lord, Mary poured forth her praise and exaltation of the Savior.

1. 'Mary rising up went into the hill country with haste into a city of Judah' (Lk. 1:39). The consent of the Blessed Virgin to become the Mother of God being received, the Angel asked for heavenly things. Mary followed the Angel and hastened to the mountain.

2. 'Mary entered the house of Zachary, and saluted Elizabeth' (Luke 1:40). Salutation is the desire of salvation. Moreover, it pertains to fraternal love to wish the salvation of our neighbor; because this is the true manner of loving our neighbor as expressed by St. Matthew, 'thou shalt love thy neighbor as thyself' (Mt. 22:29).

3. Mary said, 'My soul doth magnify the Lord.' That canticle is a canticle of praise and exultation, which each holy soul, after conceiving the word of God, can sing. What does it mean to magnify God? The Lord is magnified, not that human praise adds anything to Him; but that He may be praised in us, and our souls created to the image of God, may through justice conform themselves to Christ, who is the likeness of the Father. St. Bede beautifully says, 'Mary's soul magnifies God, because her every affection for man is transferred to God, by divine praise and service.'"[1]

Virtue to be Prayed for -- Charity

"1. Charity is the greatest amongst the theological virtues.

Ain Karem - a pretty village in the Judaean hills five miles from Jerusalem to which Mary made her way to visit her cousin Elizabeth (LK. 1: 39-56).

Ain Karem - a grotto to preserve the memory of the house of Elizabeth. This is a holy place where one can meditate on Mary meeting Elizabeth and reciting her Magnificat.

The love of charity is about that which is already possessed, since the beloved is, in a manner, in the lover, and again the lover is drawn to desire to union with the beloved; wherefore it is written, 'He that abideth in charity, abideth in God, and God in him.'

2. Charity is the form and root of all the virtues.

Now it is clear that it is charity which directs the acts of all other virtues to their last end; for the last and principal good of man is the enjoyment of God. Charity is called the mother of the other virtues, because by commanding them it conceived the acts of the other virtues by the desire of the last end.

3. Charity is caused in us by infusion.

Charity is a friendship of man for God, founded upon the fellowship of everlasting happiness. Charity can be in us neither naturally nor through acquisition by the natural powers, but by the infusion of the Holy Spirit, who is the love of the Father and the Son and the participation of whom in us is created charity.

God is supremely lovable in Himself, inasmuch as He is the object of happiness. But He is not supremely lovable to us in this way, on account of the inclination of our appetite towards visible goods. Hence it is evident that for us to love God above all things in this way, it is necessary that charity be infused into our hearts."[2]

Teachings of Vatican II

She is "the mother of the members of Christ...having cooperated by charity that faithful might be born in the Church, who are members of that Head." Wherefore she is hailed as a pre-eminent exemplar and singular member of the Church, and as its type and excellent exemplar in faith and charity.[3]

Catechism of the Catholic Church

"Called in the Gospels "the mother of Jesus," Mary is acclaimed by Elizabeth, at the prompting of the Spirit and even before the birth of her son, as "the mother of my Lord"[144] (No. 495).

Chapter 10

3. The Birth of Jesus

According to the Gospel of St. Matthew
(Chp. 1:18-25)

NOW THE BIRTH of Jesus Christ took place in this way. When his mother Mary had been betrothed to Joseph, before they came together she was found to be with child of the Holy Spirit; and her husband Joseph, being a just man and unwilling to put her to shame, resolved to send her away quietly. But as he considered this, behold, an angel of the Lord appeared to him in a dream, saying, "Joseph, son of David, do not fear to take Mary your wife, for that which is conceived in her is of the Holy Spirit; she will bear a son, and you shall call his name Jesus, for he will save his people from their sins." All this took place to fulfill what the Lord had spoken by the prophet:

"Behold, a virgin shall conceive and bear a son, and his name shall be called Emmanuel" (which means God with us). When Joseph woke from sleep, he did as the angel of the Lord commanded him; he took his wife, but knew her not until she had borne a son; and he called his name Jesus.

According to the Gospel of St. Luke
(Chp. 2:1-20)

In those days a decree went out from Caesar Augustus that all the world should be enrolled. This was the first enrollment, when Quirinius was governor of Syria. And all went to be enrolled, each to his own city. And Joseph also went up from Galilee from the city of Nazareth, to Judea, to the city of David, which is called Bethlehem, because he was of the house and lineage of David, to be enrolled with Mary, his betrothed, who was with child. And while they were there, the time came for her to be delivered. And she gave birth to her first-born son and wrapped him in swaddling cloths, and laid him in a manger, because there was no place for them in the inn. And in that region there were shepherds out in the field, keeping watch over their flocks by night. And an angel of the Lord appeared to them, and the glory of the Lord shone around them, and they were filled with fear. And the angel said to them, "Be not afraid; for behold, I bring you good news of a great joy which will come to all the people; for to you is born this day in the city of David, a Savior, who is Christ the Lord. And this will be a sign for you; you will find a babe wrapped in swaddling cloths and lying in a manger." And suddenly there was with the angel a multitude of the heavenly host praising God and saying, "Glory to God in the highest, and on earth peace among men with whom he is pleased!" When the angels went away from them into heaven, the shepherds said to one another, "Let us go over to Bethlehem and see this thing that has happened, which the Lord has made known to us." And they went with haste and found Mary and Joseph, and the babe lying in a manger. And when they saw it they made known the saying which had been told concerning this child; and all who heard it wondered at what the shepherds told them. But Mary kept all these things, pondering them in her heart. And the shepherds returned, glorifying and praising God for all they had heard and seen, as it had been told them.

According to the Gospel of St. Matthew
(Chp. 2:1-12)

Now when Jesus was born in Bethlehem of Judea in the days of

Bethlehem is six miles from Jerusalem. The Basilica of the Nativity encloses the cave in which Jesus was born.

John Paul II prays in the Cave of the Nativity on March 22, 2000. On the silver star under the altar are the words in Latin: "Here Jesus Christ was born of the Virgin Mary."

Shepherd's Field - a cave (above) where the shepherds used to spend their nights. This chapel honors the appearance and message of the angels (LK 2: 8-14).

Herod the king, behold, wise men from the East came to Jerusalem, saying, "Where is he who has been born king of the Jews? For we have seen his star in the East, and have come to worship him." When Herod the king heard this, he was troubled, and all Jerusalem with him; and assembling all the chief priests and scribes of the people, he inquired of them where the Christ was to be born. They told him, "In Bethlehem of Judea; for so it is written by the prophet: And you, O Bethlehem, in the land of Judah, are by no means least among the rulers of Judah; for from you shall come my people Israel."

Then Herod summoned the wise men secretly and ascertained from them what time the star appeared; and he sent them to Bethlehem, saying, "Go and search diligently for the child, and when you have found him bring me word, that I too may come and worship him." When they had heard the king they went their way; and lo, the star which they had seen in the East went before them, till it came to rest over the place where the child was. When they saw the star, they rejoiced exceedingly with great joy; and going into the house they saw the child with Mary his mother, and they fell down and worshipped him. Then, opening their treasures, they offered him gifts, gold and frankincense and myrrh. And being warned in a dream not to return to Herod, they departed to their own country by another way.

Consideration of the Birth of Our Lord

"1. Christ willed to be born at Bethlehem because of two reasons. First, because 'He was made of the seed of David according to the flesh, to whom also a special promise was made concerning Christ' (Rom. 1:3). Hence, He willed to be born at Bethlehem, where David was born, in order that by the very birthplace, the promise made to David might be fulfilled.

Secondly, because as St. Gregory says, 'Bethlehem is interpreted 'the house of bread'. It is Christ Himself, who said, 'I am the living Bread which came down from heaven.'

Christ chose Bethlehem for His birthplace and Jerusalem for the scene of His Passion. Likewise, also, He silenced the vain boasting of men who take pride in being born in great cities, where also they desire especially to receive honor. Christ willed to be born in a mean city and to suffer reproach in a great city.

2. Christ was born at a suitable time.

Christ as Lord and Maker of all time, chose a time in which to be born, just as He chose a mother and a birthplace. At Christ's time the whole world lived under one ruler, peace abounded on earth. Therefore it was a fitting time for the birth of Christ, for 'He is our peace, who hath made both one,' as it is written (Eph. 11:14).

Christ wished to be born when the light of day begins to increase in length, so as to show that He came in order that man might come nearer to the Divine Light according to Luke 1:79: 'to enlighten them that sit in darkness and in the shadow of death.'

In like manner, He chose to be born in the rough winter season, that He might begin from then to suffer in body for us."[1]

"Concerning the blessings and usefulness of our Savior's birth, Isaiah 11:6 says, 'A child is born to us,' that is for our benefit and welfare. In truth, there are four great blessings which have come down to us from the birth of Christ, which we may consider from the four special virtues which children possess; namely, purity, humility, lovableness, and pleasingness. These are found in the Christ Child in a most excellent manner.

First, Christ demonstrated His purity in being conceived and born without sin. We find in Him the greatest purity because He is the brightness of eternal life, and the unspotted mirror of God's majesty and the image of His goodness (Wis.6:26).

Secondly, in this Child, we find the greatest humility, for 'He, God, emptied Himself, taking the form of a slave' (Phil.2:7). He showed this humility, as St. Bernard says, in being born in a stable, wrapped in swaddling clothes, and laid in a manger.

Thirdly, we find in the Christ Child the highest kind of lovableness. He was the most beautiful of the sons of men and the delight of the Angels. The union of His Divinity with the humanity caused this lovableness in a certain manner.

Fourthly, we find in the Christ Child the greatest pleasingness for, 'He is gracious and merciful, patient and rich in mercy, and ready to repent of evil' (Joel 11:13). Wherefore, St. Bernard says, 'Christ is a child and is easily pleased. Who does not know that a child easily gives? Behold if Christ were not great and kind to us, we could never be reconciled to Him in the least thing; but the least thing, I say, done for Him is pleasing to Him.'[2]

"Christ's birth was first made known to the shepherds on the very day He was born. In order were the Magi, who came to Christ on the thirteenth day after His birth, on which day the feast of the Epiphany is celebrated. The first announcement of the grace of Christ was made by Him and His Apostles to the Jews and afterwards to the Gentiles, so the first to come to Christ were the shepherds, who were the first fruits of the Jews as being near to Him; and afterwards came the Magi from afar, who were "the first fruits of the Gentiles."[3]

"The faith of the Magi was marvelous. They sought a heavenly King, though they found in Him no sign of royal pre-eminence, yet, content with the testimony of the star alone, they adored; for they saw a man, and acknowledged a God. Moreover, they offer gifts in keeping with Christ's greatness: Gold, as to the great King; incense, as to God, because it is used in the Divine Sacrifice; and myrrh, which is used in embalming the bodies of the dead, is offered as to Him, who is to die for the salvation of all. 'All falling down they adored Him' (Mt. 2:11).

A true desire when fulfilled delights the soul. Hence the Magi who sought Christ with a more fervent desire found Him to be more delightful. Wherefore, Mt. 2:10 says: 'seeing the star, they rejoiced, with exceedingly great joy.' Thereupon, St. Bernard says, 'We rejoice with great joy when we rejoice for the sake of God and this is true joy.'

'And falling down they adored Him (Mt. 2:11). Hence, St. Augustine says, 'Oh Infancy, which even the stars obey. Whose supernatural glory and magnitude is this? That even the Angels rejoice at thy swaddling clothes and kings fear and wise men adore? Who is this that is so worshipped and so great? I am astonished when I see the swaddling clothes and behold heaven. I am inflamed with love and amazed when I see thee, poor in a manger and resplendent above the stars of Heaven. May faith help us, O Lord, where reason fails us."[4]

Virtue to be Prayed for -- Humility

"1. The Lord showed how we are to arrive at heavenly glory by the road of humility. 'And Jesus calling unto Him a little child, set him in the midst of them.' What example does this little child teach us? St. John Chrysostom believes that the child was little, since He was free from passions. Secondly, Christ called a little child, stood him in the midst of His disciples and said, 'unless you become as this little child (innocent, pure, good, free from sin), you cannot enter the kingdom of Heaven.' Thirdly, through the example of this little child is understood the Holy Spirit, because he is the spirit of humility.

The characteristics of children are many. They are immune from the lusts of the flesh. We must be imitators of the virtues and qualities of little children. And again, Christ teaches the necessity of humility saying, 'whosoever therefore, should humble himself as this little child, he is the greater in heaven. And he that shall receive one such little child in My Name, receiveth Me (Mt. 18:54)."[5]

We have the shining example of Christ's humility in His Incarnation, 'Who being in the form of God, thought it not robbery to be equal to God; but emptied Himself, taking the form of a servant.'

Beautifully indeed has it been said, "He emptied Himself,' for emptiness is the opposite of fullness. The Divine Nature was sufficiently perfect, because it contains every perfection of goodness. But human nature and the soul do not possess fullness, they are in potency or in power to possess fullness; for they are as it were a tabula rasa, an empty tablet. Hence human nature is empty. Therefore it is well, 'He emptied Himself,' for He assumed human nature.

'Taking the form of a servant.' For man is by creation the servant of God and human nature is the form of a servant.

2. The example of Christ in His Passion is an example of humility. 'He humbled Himself, becoming obedient unto death, even unto the death of the cross.' Christ is man, but exceedingly great, because He is at the same time God and man and still He humbled Himself. But the manner of humiliation and the sign of humility is obedience.

But how did He become obedient? Not by His Divine Will, for that is a rule, but by His human will which was ruled in all things according to the will of the heavenly Father. The movement of the human will tends to two things, to life and to honor. But Christ was not unwilling to die. Likewise He did not flee from the shameful death of the cross."[6]

Teachings of John Paul II

"The Nativity brings us within touching distance, so to speak, of our spiritual birth in God through grace. Born through faith and grace, we have been called children of God; and so we are, says St. John."[7]

Catechism of the Catholic Church

"Jesus was born in a humble stable into a poor family.[202] Simple shepherds were the first witnesses to this event (No. 525). To become a child in relation to God is the condition for entering the kingdom.[205] For this, we must humble ourselves and become little" (No. 526).

Chapter 11

4. The Presentation of Jesus in the Temple

According to the Gospel of St. Luke
(Chp. 2:22-40)

AND WHEN THE time came for their purification according to the Law of Moses, they brought him up to Jerusalem to present him to the Lord (as it is written in the Law of the Lord, "every male that opens the womb shall be called holy to the Lord"). And to offer a sacrifice according to what is said in the Law of the Lord, "a pair of turtle-doves, or two young pigeons."

Now there was a man in Jerusalem, whose name was Simeon, and this man was righteous and devout, looking for the consolation of Israel, and the Holy Spirit was upon him. And it had been revealed to him by the Holy Spirit that he should not see death before he had seen the Lord's Christ. And inspired by the Spirit he came into the Temple; and when the parents brought in the Child Jesus, to do for him according to the custom of the Law, he took him up in his arms and blessed God and said,

"Lord, now lettest thou thy servant depart in peace, according to thy word; for mine eyes have seen they salvation which thou hast prepared in the presence of all peoples, a light for revelation to the Gentiles, and for glory to thy people Israel." And his father and his mother marvelled at what was said about him; and Simeon blessed them and said to Mary his mother, "Behold, this child is set for the fall and rising of many in Israel, and for a sign that is spoken against and a sword will pierce through your own soul also, that thoughts out of many hearts may be revealed."

Consideration of the Presentation of the Child Jesus in the Temple

After the days of her purification, according to the Law of Moses were accomplished, they carried Him to Jerusalem, to present Him to the Lord" (Lk. 2:22).

"Now the Law contained a two-fold precept relating to children born. One was a general precept which referred to all—namely, that 'when the days of the mother's purification had expired,' a sacrifice was to be offered either 'for a son or for a daughter,' as laid down in Lev. 12:6. And this sacrifice was for the expiation of the sin in which the child was conceived and born and also for a certain consecration of the child, because it was then presented in the Temple for the first time.

The other was a special precept in the Law concerning the first-born of both 'man and beast'; for the Lord claimed for Himself all the first-born in Israel, because in order to deliver the Israelites, He 'slew every first-born in the land of Egypt, both men and cattle,' (Ex. 12:12) the first-born of Israel being saved; which Law is set down in Ex. 13. Here also Christ was foreshadowed, who is the "First-born amongst many brethren' (Rom. 8:29).

Therefore, since Christ was born of a woman and was her first-born and since He wished to be 'made under the Law,' the Evangelist Luke shows that both these precepts were fulfilled in His regard. First, as to that which concerns the first-born when he says: 'They carried Him to Jerusalem to present Him to the Lord; as it is written in the Law of the Lord, 'Every male opening the womb shall be called holy to the Lord' (Lk. 2:22-23).

*On March 26, 2000, John Paul II prayed at the Wailing Wall
in Jerusalem, the most imposing remains of the Temple where
Jesus' presentation took place.*

'And to offer a sacrifice according as it is written in the Law of the Lord, pair of turtle doves or two young pigeons' (Luke 2:24).[1]

'After the days of her purification according to the Law of Moses were accomplished, they carried Him to Jerusalem, to present Him to the Lord' (Luke 2:22). In this Gospel, seven virtues are to be observed in the Blessed Virgin. First, humility in her purification since she did not need purification; second, love of purity in her superabundant purification; third, love of obedience according to the Law; fourth, reverence to her Son in bringing Him to Jerusalem; fifth, devotion in visiting the Holy place; sixth, thanksgiving in the oblation of her Son, 'So that they might present Him to the Lord, we offer to Thee O Lord, Him whom Thou has given to us.' Seventh, poverty in the offering, namely two doves, which was the offering of the poor."[2]

The Virtue to be Prayed for -- Justice

"1. It seems to belong to justice that each one pays his debt. Because of the diverse nature of the debt, different virtues are employed; for example, religion by which a debt is paid to God, loyalty by which a debt is rendered to our parents and to our country, thanksgiving by which we render a debt to our benefactors, and so on concerning other virtues. And there is legal justice which is called a general virtue as it directs all the virtues to the common good. But in addition to justice which intends the common good, there is another justice properly called, which is intended for the private good of each one, so that what belongs to each one may be rendered to him.

2. The precepts of the Decalogue are precepts of justice. The Precepts of the Decalogue are the first principles of the Law and the natural reason assents to them at once as to principles that are most evident. Now it is altogether evident that the idea of duty, which is essential to a precept, appears in justice that is towards another. The precepts of the Decalogue need to pertain to justice. Wherefore, the first precepts are about acts of religion which is the chief part of

justice, the fourth precept is about acts of piety which is the second part of justice, and the six remaining are about justice commonly so called which is observed among equals."[3]

Teachings of John Paul II

"The Presentation is the first of the events which clearly reveal the messianic status of the new-born child. With him are linked the fall and the rising of many in the old Israel and also the new. The cost of the cross was shared by the mother, whose soul—according to Simeon's words—was to be pierced by a sword, 'so that the thoughts of many hearts might be laid bare.'"[4]

Catechism of the Catholic Church

"The *presentation of Jesus in the temple* shows him to be the first born Son who belongs to the Lord.[216] With Simeon and Anna, all Israel awaits its *encounter* with the Savior–the name given to this event in the Byzantine tradition" (No. 529).

Chapter 12

5. *The Finding of the Child Jesus in the Temple*

According to the Gospel of St. Luke
(Chp. 2:41-52)

NOW HIS PARENTS went to Jerusalem every year at the feast of the Passover. And when he was twelve years old, they went up according to custom; and when the feast was ended, as they were returning, the boy Jesus stayed behind in Jerusalem. His parents did not know it, but supposing him to be in the company, they went a day's journey, and they sought him among their kinsfolk and acquaintances; and when they did not find him, they returned to Jerusalem seeking him. After three days they found him in the temple, sitting among the teachers, listening to them and asking them questions; and all who heard him were amazed at his understanding and his answers. And when they saw him they were astonished; and his mother said to him, "Son, why have you treated us so? Behold, your father and I have been looking for you anxiously." And he said to them, "How is it that you sought me? Did you not know that I must be in my Father's house?" And they did not understand the saying which he spoke to them.

And he went down with them and came to Nazareth, and was obedient to them; and his mother kept all these things in her heart. And Jesus increased in wisdom and in stature, and in favour with God and man.

Consideration of the Finding
of Jesus in the Temple

"Thy father and I have sought Thee, sorrowing." (Luke 2:48)

"From these words we learn to seek God, and Sacred Scripture often advises us to search for Him. Moreover, three things are here to be observed: Those searching; a manner of searching; and God whom we must seek.

First, those searching are Mary and Joseph. 'I and the father,' by whom two kinds are meant who seek the Lord. He is sought for by contemplatives in meditation and by men of action in their works. By Mary is represented the enlightened and she also signifies the contemplatives who in meditation receive divine illuminations. Joseph signifies an increase of the works of mercy and represents the active (those living an active life) who should have an increase of the works of mercy. The Lord is sought by these two classes of people.

Secondly, concerning the manner of seeking the Lord. He should be sought in six ways. 1. With purity of mind, so that we should be free from every stain of sin. 2. With simplicity of intention. 3. With the will, so that we may think of God only. 4. With haste before the time passes in which God cannot be found. 5. With perseverance and 6. Without ceasing and with sorrow for sin.

Thirdly, we should seek God since it is written, 'Thy father and I have sought Thee.' Moreover, He must be sought by us for four reasons, because He is just, meek, good, and He is Life. Just, for He offers Himself to those seeking Him and in this way His justice is manifested for not one seeks God as He should be sought but finds Him. Meek, for those seeking God, as those who seek Him, He magnifies and rewards. Life, because those who seek God, He makes them live eternally."[1]

Virtue to be Prayed for -- Prudence

"1. A prudent man is one who is capable of taking good counsel. A prudent man is one who disposes well of the things that have to be done for a good end; whoever disposes well of such things as are fitting for an evil end has false prudence, in so far as that which he takes for an end is good, not in truth but *in* appearance.

2. True and perfect prudence takes counsel, judges and commands aright in respect to the good end of man's whole life, and this alone is prudence simply so called.

3. Cicero rightly divides prudence into memory of the past, knowledge of the present and foreknowledge of the future. For prudence is concerned about particular works, and the prudent man reasons rightly concerning these things which he must do, that from the things which exist and which he keeps in memory and from the things which his intellect considers, he provides for the future. For memory is that faculty by which the mind reflects or recalls those things which happen, intelligence that faculty by which one examines those things which exist, while foreknowledge is that by which some future event is seen before it happens."[2]

Catechism of the Catholic Church

"The *finding of Jesus in the temple* is the only event that breaks the silence of the Gospels about the hidden years of Jesus.[226] Here Jesus lets us catch a glimpse of the mystery of his total consecration to a mission that flows from his divine sonship: "Did you not know that I must be about my Father's work?"[227] Mary and Joseph did not understand these words, but they accepted them in faith. Mary "kept all these things in her heart" during the years Jesus remained hidden in the silence of an ordinary life" (No. 534).

Chapter 13

1. The Agony in the Garden

According to the Gospel of St. Luke
(Chp. 22:39-46)

AND HE CAME out, and went, as was his custom, to the Mount of Olives; and the disciples followed him. And when he came to the place he said, "Pray that you may not enter into temptation." And he withdrew from them about a stone's throw, and knelt down and prayed, "Father, if thou are willing, remove this cup from me, nevertheless not my will, but thine, be done." And there appeared to him an angel from heaven, strengthening him. And being in agony he prayed more earnestly; and his sweat became like great drops of blood falling upon the ground. And when he rose from prayer, he came to the disciples and found them sleeping for sorrow, and he said to them, "Why do you sleep? Rise and pray that you may not enter into temptation."

Consideration of the Agony in the Garden

"A threefold condition for prayer is recommended by Our Divine

*The Garden of Gethsemane, with 8 olive trees still standing,
is where Jesus spent perhaps the most sorrowful hours
of his Passion.*

On March 25, 2000, John Paul II prays in the Basilica of the Agony. This is the rock where Jesus sweat blood.

Lord, namely, carefulness, humility and devotion.

First, *carefulness*, in going a little further, because He withdrew even from those whom He had chosen. 'When you pray, enter your room, and having closed the door, pray to thy Father in secret.' Our Lord advanced not a great deal, but a little, so that the Apostles might see Him praying and might acquire a method of praying.

Second, *humility* —'He fell upon His face.' By this, Christ left us an example of humility. First, because humility is necessary for prayer, and because Peter had said, 'If I should die with Thee, I will not deny thee.' Therefore the Lord continued to pray so that neither the Apostles, nor we, might depend too much upon our own power.

Third, *devotion* is shown when He said: 'My Father,' etc. It is necessary for a person praying to pray devotionally. Hence He said, 'My Father,' because Christ is the Son of the Father by nature, and we are sons by adoption.

'If it be possible, let this chalice pass from Me. Nevertheless not as I will, but as Thou wilt.' Here is set forth the power of every good and persevering prayer. Christ prayed according to His affection, in as far as His prayer expressed the affections of His sensitive nature. He did this to teach us three things:

First, that He might prove He assumed a true human nature with all its natural affections. Second, that he might show that it is not lawful for man to wish what the Lord does not wish. Third, that He might teach us to subject our affections to the Divine Will.

Christ, acting as man, manifested a human will when He said: 'Let this chalice pass from me,' for He was then wishing for something human. But because He wished His desire to be directed to God, Christ added: 'However, not as I will, but as Thou wilt.' Christ had two wills, one from the Father, as He was God; the other a human will as He was man, and He submitted to the Father this will in all things so that we might submit our wills to the holy will of God in all things. 'I came down from Heaven, not to do My own will, but the will of the Father who sent Me'."[1]

Virtue to be Prayed for -- Religion

"Religion directs man to God. For it is He to whom we ought to be bound as to our unfailing principle; to whom also our choice should be resolutely directed as to our last end; and whom when we neglect Him by sinning, we should recover by believing and practicing our faith. Now the good to which religion is directed is to give due honor to God."[2]

"*Devotion* is in truth an interior act of religion. Devotion means to will to give oneself readily to things pertaining to the service of God. Charity causes devotion, inasmuch as love makes one ready to serve one's friend, and at the same time charity feeds on devotion. Meditation is also the cause of devotion. St. Augustine says that 'the will arises from the intelligence.' Consequently meditation must be the cause of devotion, insofar as through meditation man conceives the thought of surrendering himself to God's service. Two considerations help lead a person to God's service. The first is the consideration of God's goodness and loving kindness. This consideration arouses love, which is the proximate cause of devotion.

The second consideration is that of man's own shortcomings on account of which he needs to lean on God. Science and anything else conducive to greatness is to man an occasion of self-confidence, so that he does not entirely surrender himself to God. The result is that such like things sometimes occasion a hindrance to devotion; while in simple souls devotion abounds by repressing pride. If, however, a man perfectly submits to God his science or any other perfection, by this very fact his devotion is increased.

The direct and principal effect of devotion is the spiritual joy of the mind. The consideration of God's goodness causes devotion and the direct result of this consideration is joy.

Prayer is an act of religion. It belongs properly to religion to show reverence and honor to God, and therefore all those things through which reverence is shown to God, pertain to religion. Now man shows reverence to God by means of prayer, insofar as man subjects himself to God, and by praying acknowledges that he needs Him as the Author of his good. By praying, man surrenders his mind to God, since he subjects it to Him and so to speak presents it to Him. Prayer, which belongs to the intellect, is the chief of the acts of religion, for by prayer religion directs man's intellect to God.

Devout prayer obtains for us a threefold good. First, it is an efficacious and useful remedy against evils. Second, it is powerful and useful in obtaining what we ask. Third, prayer makes us friends of God."[3]

Prayer consists of meditation and contemplation

"Meditating on matters pertaining to Christ's humanity is the strongest incentive to love and consequently to devotion, leading us as a guiding hand. For the works of God must be meditated on because they are profound. The mysteries of God and His works are also delightful for meditation and frequent reflection. They also are useful to us as subjects for contemplation because they lead us to a knowledge of their Author. If anyone from a devout intention meditates on the suitableness of Christ's passion and death, he will find such depth of wisdom, that certain things will always suggest more and greater things to every reflecting mind."[4]

"Prayers should be vocal, for three reasons. First, in order to excite interior devotion. St. Augustine says that 'by means of words and other signs we arouse ourselves more sharply to an increase of holy desires.' Second, the voice is used as though to pay it as debt so that man may serve God with all that he has from God, not only with his mind but also with his body. Third, we have recourse to vocal prayer, through a certain overflow from the soul into the body, from an excess of feeling."[5]

Unanswered prayer

"Do we always ask something pertaining to the good of our soul, or do we sometimes seek only material things which if granted might ruin our souls, because of the improper use we might possibly make of God's gifts? It happens then that one might ask something from God, which does not pertain to his salvation. We might do this in two ways. First, from a wrong disposition of mind, for example when we seek something which we like, but which if obtained, might be injurious to our salvation. For the good Lord sometimes refuses to grant that which we ask, so that He may grant something more beneficial to us later on. Secondly, we might ask something from ignorance, as when we ask that which we think is useful for us but which is not. God who is more wise than we are, does not grant those things which He foresees would be a disadvantage to us.

Sometimes Christ puts off granting what we ask, to increase our desire to pray, and so that He might grant our request at a more suitable time.

It also happens sometimes, that we ask from God a favor for another, but we are not heard because of the sins of that person. Human perversity, a desire to continue to sin, the actual perseverance in sin on the part of that person stand in the way of our prayer and of our request being granted. St. Monica had to pray many years for her wayward son Augustine, before she saw him converted, or before the desired effect of her prayers was really granted. Hence we must pray perseveringly, humbly, confidently, fervently and in the name of Christ, leaving it to Him to grant or not grant our requests as He sees fit, and in His own time and manner."[6]

Teachings of Vatican II

"The Christian is indeed called to pray with his brethren, but he must also enter into his chamber to pray to the Father, in secret; yet more, according to the teaching of the Apostle, he should pray without ceasing."[7]

Teachings of John Paul II

"Gethsemane: a place of intense loneliness for Jesus, of almost total dereliction as he faced his Passion. The inner reality of Jesus' agony in Gethsemane remained hidden from his disciples, who in any case had fallen asleep from emotional exhaustion. But let us not forget that when he broke off from prayer he said to Peter: 'Watch and pray, so that you may not enter into temptation' (Mk 14:38)."[8]

Catechism of the Catholic Church

"Jesus prays: "My Father, if it be possible, let this cup pass from me . . ."[435] Thus he expresses the horror that death represented for his human nature. Like ours, his human nature is destined for eternal life; but unlike ours, it is perfectly exempt from sin, the cause of death"[436] (No. 612).

Chapter 14

2. The Scourging at the Pillar

According to the Gospel of St. Luke
(Chp. 22:47-53)

WHILE HE WAS still speaking, there came a crowd, and the man called Judas, one of the twelve, was leading them. He drew near to Jesus to kiss him; but Jesus said to him, "Judas, would you betray the Son of man with a kiss?" And when those who were about him saw what would follow, they said, "Lord, shall we strike with the sword?" And one of them struck the slave of the high priest and cut off his right ear. But Jesus said, "No more of this!" And he touched his ear and healed him. Then Jesus said to the chief priests and captains of the temple and elders, who had come out against him, "Have you come out as against a robber, with swords and clubs? When I was with you day after day in the temple, you did not lay hands on me. But this is your hour, and the power of darkness.

Chp. 23:1-5

Then the whole company of them arose, and brought him before Pilate. And they began to accuse him, saying, "We found this man perverting our nation, and forbidding us to give tribute to Caesar, and saying that he himself is Christ a king." And Pilate asked him, "Are you the King of the Jews?" And he answered him, "You have

156

said so." And Pilate said to the chief priests and the multitudes, "I find no crime in this man." But they were urgent saying, "He stirs up the people, teaching throughout all Judea, from Galilee even to this place."

According to the Gospel of St. Matthew
(Chp. 27:15-26)

Now at the feast, the governor was accustomed to release for the crowd any one prisoner whom they wanted. And they had then a notorious prisoner, called Barabbas. So when they had gathered, Pilate said to them, "Whom do you want me to release for you, Barabbas or Jesus who is called Christ?" For he knew that it was out of envy that they had delivered him up. Besides, while he was sitting on the judgment seat, his wife sent word to him, "Have nothing to do with that righteous man, for I have suffered much over him today in a dream." Now the chief priests and the elders persuaded the people to ask for Barabbas and destroy Jesus. The governor again said to them, "Which of the two do you want me to release for you?" And they said, "Barabbas." Pilate said to them, "Then what shall I do with Jesus who is called Christ?" They all said, "Let him be cruci-fied." And he said, "Why, what evil has he done?" But they shouted all the more, "Let him be crucified."

So when Pilate saw that he was gaining nothing, but rather that a riot was beginning, he took water and washed his hands before the crowd, saying, "I am innocent of this righteous man's blood; see to it yourselves." And all the people answered, "His blood be on us and on our children!" Then he released for them Barabbas, and having scourged Jesus, delivered him to be crucified.

Consideration of the Scourging at the Pillar

"Why did Pilate deliver Jesus to be crucified? St. Jerome says, 'it was the custom among the Romans; that anyone sentenced to death, should first be scourged.' Some say that Pilate scourged Jesus to move the multitude to compassion so that the rabble in seeing Jesus scourged, might let Him go free. He scourged Him, not with His own hands, but through the rough hands of unmerciful soldiers. This was ordered done, so that the Jews observing His injuries, might be satisfied and might desist from putting Jesus to death.

"For it is natural for angry persons to cease from their rage when they see him humiliated and punished, against whom their anger is aroused. It is characteristic of anger that it desires an injury to its neighbor with moderation; but not so with actual hate, which desires the complete destruction of the person held in hatred. Moreover, the enemies of Christ were moved with actual hatred against Christ.

"But does this intention excuse Pilate from his crime in the scourging of Christ? By no means, because of all things which are directly bad in themselves, none can become entirely good by a good intention. Moreover to punish the innocent and especially to punish the Son of God, is in itself the greatest evil and therefore, in no way, can it be excused or exonerated from blame."[1]

Virtue to be Prayed for -- Temperance

"The word temperance means a certain temperateness or moderation which reason appoints to human operations and passions and this is common to every moral virtue. Temperance withdraws man from things which seduce the appetite from obeying reason and the Divine Law.

"Temperance is concerned chiefly about pleasures and desires of touch, secondarily, it is about other desires. St. Augustine says that, 'the function of temperance is to control and quell the desires which draw us to the things which withdraw us from the laws of God, and from the fruit of His goodness, and it is the duty of temperance to spurn all bodily allurement and popular praise.'

"The good of moral virtue consists chiefly in the order of reason, because man's good is to be in accord with right reason. Temperance takes the need of this life as the rule of the pleasurable objects of which it makes use, and uses them only as much as the need of this life requires.

"Although beauty is becoming to every virtue, it is attributed to temperance by way of excellence for two reasons. First, in regard to the general notion of temperance, which consists in a certain moderate and fitting proportion, and this is what we understand by beauty.

"Secondly, because the things from which temperance withholds us, hold the lowest place in man and are becoming to him by reason of his animal nature, wherefore it is natural that such things should defile him. In consequence, beauty is a foremost attribute of temperance, which above all hinders man from being defiled, for temperance destroys the things which degrade man and withstands the vices that bring most dishonor on man."[2]

Teachings of John Paul II

"For many people the scourging of the Lord became the decisive reason for their determination to break the bonds of sin, the reason for mortifying the concupiscence of the flesh, for turning their desires toward the noble and holy.

"Let us remember that the Savior's bloody Passion began when the scouring was inflicted. The flaying at the hands of the soldiers literally drew blood. The maddened crowd shouted, 'His blood be upon us and upon our children' (Mt. 27:25)."[3]

Chapter 15

3. The Crowning with Thorns

According to the Gospel of St. Matthew
(Chp. 27:27-31)

THEN THE SOLDIERS of the governor took Jesus into the pra etorium, and they gathered the whole battalion before him. And they stripped him and put a scarlet robe upon him, and plaiting a crown of thorns they put it on his head, and put a reed in his right hand. And kneeling before him they mocked him, saying, "Hail, King of the Jews!" And they spat upon him, and took the reed and struck him on the head. And when they had mocked him, they stripped him of the robe, and put his own clothes on him, and led him away to crucify him.

Consideration of the Crowning with Thorns

"Jesus was crowned with thorns in cruelty and derision, but the painful crown by which He expiated for our sins of pride flowered into a crown of glory for Him as the King of kings and Lord of lords. And Mary, who saw Him go by bearing His crown of thorns, became associated with Him in His glory. Before having her share in His final victory, our Lord allied her with Him in His sufferings, in the intimate peace that continued in the depth of their hearts in spite of everything, and in His desire to be immolated as a perfect holocaust for the salvation of man. The demon, who is pride personified, suffers more by being vanquished by Mary's humility than if he were immediately put down by the all-powerful God.

The humbled and thorn-crowned Jesus will be uplifted above all. 'He humbled Himself, becoming obedient unto death, even to the death of the cross.'"[1]

Virtue to be Prayed for -- Love of our Enemies

"It is clear that you sin if you do not grant pardon to the person who has injured or offended you. It is Christian charity that we love such persons, attract them to God, and let them share in our friendship, and many reasons induce us to do this.

"We should love our enemies in order to preserve our own dignity as Christians. Among all the signs of dignity, the greatest is that we are children of God. The sign of this dignity is that you love your enemies. 'Love your enemies so that you may be children of your Father who is in Heaven' (Mt. 5:44). If we love only our friends, that is not a sign of our divine affliction, for even sinners to this!

"There is the victory which we achieve from loving our enemies. Everyone naturally desires to be a winner and to secure the prize of victory. But to be victorious in this contest over self, you must attract him who has offended you; attract him to love by your own goodness; for if you entertain hatred against your offender you lose. 'Be not overcome by evil, but overcome evil by good' (Rom. 12:21).

"There is the good and far-reaching example resulting from the love we show our enemies. Through this means you make friends. There can be no greater incentive to love than to love one's enemy for the love of God. No one is so hardhearted that even if he is unwilling to manifest love, still he is attracted by love.

"Our prayers are more easily and quickly answered if we forgive our enemies who may have offended, insulted, or injured us.

"They who pray for their enemies will win the friendship of God for themselves and for their persecutors. St. Stephen, the martyr, did a great service to the Church when he prayed for those who stoned him to death, because through his prayers Paul was converted from a persecutor of the Church to an Apostle of Christ.

"By showing love towards our enemies we avoid a multitude of sins. God often wishes to draw us to Himself through sickness and again through persecution from our enemies. We follow the way of the Lord if we forgive our enemies. 'Forgive and you will be forgiven' (Mt. 5:7). And again Christ said: 'Blessed are the merciful, for they shall obtain mercy,' for there is no greater mercy than to pardon our enemies. 'Do good to those who hate you. Bless those who curse you and pray for those who persecute and calumniate you.' Such is God's Way and God's Law."[2]

Teachings of John Paul II

"The torture inflicted on the Savior's head was a terrible one. Pilate had him brought out for the crowd to see in just that condition, crowned with thorns; he showed them all his humiliation and said, 'Here is the man' (Jn. 19:5)."[3]

"Here we have before us the Christ in the truth of his kingship. Pilate says: 'Here is the man.' Precisely, all the kingliness of man, all man's dignity—which Jesus came to express and renew—are here summed up in him. We are reminded by the Second Vatican Council that Jesus came in order to reveal the kingliness of man. And here, visible to the whole of humanity, stands Jesus crowned with thorns! The price paid for dignity is the blood of the Son of God."[4]

Chapter 16

4. The Carrying of the Cross

According to the Gospel of St. Luke
(Chp. 23:26-32)

A ND AS THEY led him away, they seized one Simon of Cyrene, who was coming in from the country, and laid on him the cross, to carry it behind Jesus. And there followed him a great multitude of the people, and of women who bewailed and lamented him. But Jesus turning to them said, "Daughters of Jerusalem, do not weep for me, but weep for yourselves and for your children."

For behold, the days are coming when they will say, "Blessed are the barren, and the wombs that never bore, and the breasts that never gave suck! Then they will begin to say to the mountains. 'Fall on us'; and to the hills, 'Cover us.' For if they do this when the wood is green, what will happen when it is dry?" Two others also, who were criminals, were led away to be put to death with him.

Consideration of the Carrying of the Cross

"In bearing His cross Jesus makes an interior offering of Himself for us; the fullness of the gift of self is achieved in the complete sacrifice, the perfect holocaust which is about to be consumed. He was invested with the fullness of grace for the accomplishment of His mission as the redeemer of sinful mankind. This fullness of grace acted like a weight in His soul drawing Him toward Calvary; it drove deep into Him an unfathomable attraction for the cross, the ardor of His love leading Him to that sacrifice which would render all glory to God and accomplish the salvation of men: 'Love is the weight that draws me'."[1]

"Jesus falls, not because He is overcome by weariness against His will, but because His love aspires to the farthest limits of suffering that we may know His love for us. Men lay the cross upon Jesus. He is absolutely innocent; yet He sees the justice of God in men's injustice. If we who are guilty of so many hidden faults with which no one reproaches us happen to suffer some injustice from others, let us see in it God's purifying justice.

"Jesus suffered because of the sins of all men of every race and time. And His suffering was proportionate to His wisdom: He knew better than anyone else the number and gravity of men's crimes; they lay open before Him somewhat as we see the purulent sores of a body consumed with disease. Jesus' fullness of grace augmented His capacity for suffering whereas the egoism that keeps us living on the surface of ourselves, allows us to find pain only in whatever touches us personally and renders us incapable of supernatural suffering arising out of love of God and souls, an anguish unknown to superficial minds. Lord, give us sorrow for our sins."[2]

"Jesus willed to drink to the dregs the terrible chalice presented to Him in Gethsemane and containing all the shame and iniquity of the world, taking it for Himself and giving us in exchange the chalice of His precious blood, a blessed cup filled to overflowing with grace issuing from His bruised heart. In carrying the cross, he falls face downward on the ground, just as He fell in the Garden of Olives.

"What would we have said if we had met our Lord carrying His cross and He had asked us, 'Will you help Me?' Today when a cross comes to us, it is Jesus who comes, Jesus who loves us, Jesus who desires to reproduce in us His own traits, Jesus whom we love.

"We fail to realize how much we need the cross for our own purification and for the humble measure of work which God is good enough to let us do for the salvation of our neighbor. In a sense Jesus continues His agony to the end of the world in His mystical body, offering to let us help Him by carrying the cross prepared for us from all eternity and adapted by Him to our strength as sustained by His grace. We all have a cross; through contemplation and love our cross becomes healing for us and radiant for others, helping them to carry their own cross holily. We really know others only when we know the cross they carry.

"Let us ask Mary to help us understand the mystery of the cross that we may accept and carry our cross not in revolt and vexation but with thankfulness and then with love, which will keep on increasing through daily Communion, by personal merit, and by love itself, which by its own action obtains an increase of grace."[3]

"The sacred face of the Savior may be marked with bruises and spittle, but it loses nothing of its nobility and greatness and bears the reflection of His sacred soul, which even in this life contemplated the divine essence unveiled and looked upon the life of eternity to which He was leading us. But He willed to confine the light of glory to the summit of His intellect and gave Himself up to every humiliation and opportunity during that hour when Veronica came forward to wipe His blood-stained face.

"Daughters of Jerusalem, weep not for Me." I give it freely. Nothing can give you so striking a proof of My love for you as My Passion. 'Weep for yourselves.' Blessed are they who weep the holy tears of contrition. Weep not for your crosses, which serve to purify you and make you free, but weep for your sins. 'If any man will come after Me, let him take up his cross.' There is no other way to follow Me. 'Weep for your children,' for all who fail to understand, who curse and blaspheme the divine mystery of the cross."[4]

The Virtue to be Prayed for -- Fortitude

"The word fortitude can be understood in two ways. First as simply denoting a certain firmness of mind, and in this sense it is a general virtue or rather a condition of every virtue to act firmly and immovably. Secondly, fortitude may be understood to denote firmness only in bearing and withstanding these things wherein it is most difficult to be firm, namely, in certain grave dangers.

"Fortitude is chiefly concerned around the dangers of death. It belongs to the virtue of fortitude to guard the will of man and remove any obstacle that withdraws the will from following the reason, withdraws it from the good of reason because of fear of corporal evil. Now it behooves one to hold firmly the good of reason against every evil whatsoever, since no bodily good is equivalent to the good of the reason. Hence, fortitude of soul must be that which binds the will firmly to the good of reason in face of the greatest evils.

"The most fearful of all bodily evils is death since it deprives us of all bodily goods. Fortitude, therefore, consists in this, that man does not depart from the good of virtue on account of the dangers of death which seem to hang over him. Fortitude is chiefly against the dangers of death, still it is secondarily against all other dangers because a brave man behaves well in bearing all manner of adversity.

"The act of fortitude is not chiefly to attack difficult things but to endure them, that is to stand immovable in the midst of dangers rather than to attack them; to stand without the confusion resulting from irrational fear.

"First, because endurance seemingly implies that one is being attacked by a stronger person. Secondly, because he that endures already feels the presence of danger whereas the aggressor looks upon danger as something to come and it is more difficult to be unmoved by the present than by the future. Thirdly, because endurance implies length of time, and it is more difficult to remain calm and unmoved for a long time than to be moved suddenly to something arduous. Hence Aristotle says, 'that some hurry to meet danger, yet fly when the danger is present; this is not the behavior of a brave man'."[5]

Teachings of John Paul II

"And on his shoulders the full weight of the cross! A weight under which he falls. His persecutors themselves have to find someone to help him, someone who with him will carry it to the place of execution. Perhaps at this point we may visualize other men similarly burdened. Jesus of Nazareth has many Simons of Cyrene in our own century, men who are obliged, often by force to carry crosses of various kinds. Let us ask ourselves: are they carrying them with Christ?"[6]

Catechism of the Catholic Church

"The cross is the unique sacrifice of Christ, the "one mediator between God and men".[452] He calls his disciples "to take up their cross and follow him,"[454] for "Christ also suffered for us, leaving us an example so that we should follow in his steps".[455] In fact Jesus desires to associate with his redeeming sacrifice those who were to be its first beneficiaries.[456] This is achieved supremely in the case of his mother, who was associated more intimately than any other person in the mystery of his redemptive suffering"[457] (No. 618).

Chapter 17

5. *The Crucifixion and Death of Jesus*

According to the Gospel of St. Luke
(Chp. 23:33-43)

W HEN THEY REACHED the place called The Skull, they cru cified him there and the two criminals also, one on the right, the other on the left. Jesus said, "Father, forgive them; they do not know what they are doing." Then they cast lots to share out his clothing. The people stayed there watching him. As for the leaders, they jeered at him, "He saved others," they said, "let him save himself if he is the Christ of God the Chosen One." The soldiers mocked him too, and when they approached to offer him vinegar they said, "If you are the king of the Jews, save yourself." Above him there was an inscription: "This is the King of the Jews."

One of the criminals hanging there abused him. "Are you not the Christ?" he said. "Save yourself and us as well." But the other spoke up and rebuked him. "Have you no fear of God at all?" he said. "You got the same sentence as he did, but in our case we deserved it: we are paying for what we did. But this man has done nothing wrong." He then said, "Jesus, remember me when you come into your kingdom." "Indeed, I promise you," he replied "today you will be with me in paradise."

The Basilica of the Holy Sepulcher, which is called the "Mother of all Churches," holds both Calvary and the empty tomb.

On March 26, 2000, in the Basilica of the Holy Sepulcher,
John Paul II laboriously climbed the stairs leading to
Calvary. He prayed on the site where the cross was raised.

John 19:25-27

Near the cross of Jesus stood him mother and his mother's sister, Mary the wife of Clopas, and Mary of Magdala. Seeing his mother and the disciple he loved standing near her, Jesus said to his mother, "Woman, this is your son." Then to the disciple he said, "This is your mother." And from that moment the disciple made a place for her in his home.

Mark 15:33-39

When the sixth hour came there was darkness over the whole land until the ninth hour. And at the ninth hour Jesus cried out in a loud voice, "Eloi, Eloi, lama sabachthani?" which means, "My God, my God, why have you deserted me?" When some of those who stood by heard this, they said, "Listen, he is calling to Elijah." Someone ran and soaked a sponge in vinegar and putting it on a reed gave it to him to drink saying, "Wait and see if Elijah will come to take him down." But Jesus gave a loud cry and breathed his last. And the veil of the Temple was torn in two from top to bottom. The centurion, who was standing in front of him, had seen how he had died, and he said, "In truth this man was the Son of God."

Consideration of the Crucifixion

"Our Lord's garments adhere to the wounds made by the scourging and as they are torn off, His body flames with pain. This exterior and humiliating divestment symbolizes another and interior divestment which our Lord asks of us. We ought to strip ourselves of that self, compounded of egoism, self-love under its many forms and of pride, that we may be clothed with humility and divine charity, which will enlarge our hearts and give them in a sense the great heartedness of God by making us love everything as He loves it."[1]

"St. Luke tells us: "And when they came to the place called Calvary, they crucified Him there: and the robbers, one on the right hand and the other on the left. And Jesus said 'Father, forgive them...,' expressing the highest act of fortitude and meekness combined. At the moment when His executioners crucify Him He is meriting grace for them and asking the Father that they may have eternal life. If we must suffer from another, let us pray for him; if on our part we make others suffer, let us think that perhaps God inspires them to pray for us; let us remember that He most certainly prayed for us who were the cause of His death.

"Because the crucifixion was our Lord's hour, His great hour, and the highest point of the whole history of the world, let us look at every moment of our lives in relation to it, that we may be faithful to the grace of the present moment."[2]

"Our Lord's last words express deep and radiant peace. To the good thief: 'This day thou shalt be with Me in paradise': a word of peace to all great penitents, that they may know themselves pardoned. To Mary and to John: 'Woman, behold thy son . . . Behold, thy Mother': words producing what they signify, greatly increasing the Virgin's motherly love for all redeemed souls represented by the beloved Apostle.

'My God, my God, why has thou abandoned me?' is the first verse of Psalm 21, the Messianic psalm consummated in perfect abandonment by Him who restores peace to the world and bears in our stead the malediction due to sin.

'I thirst': the Savior thirsts for souls and He Himself leads them to the living water of grace to purify, refresh, and save them.

'It is consummated': the perfect holocaust prefigured by the sacrifices of the Old Law is offered; it will be perpetuated in substance in the holy Mass until the end of the world.

'Father, into thy hands I commend My spirit': these words consecrate and offer the sacrifice of the cross. Because the boundless love of the Word made flesh inspires His oblation, it has an infinitely meritorious and satisfactory value and achieves more to please God than all the sins of all men accomplish to displease Him."[3]

"Receiving into her arms the body of her Son, Mary glimpsed by faith to some extent God's infinite mercy for sinners and she adores the divine justice to which Jesus made perfect reparation. Let us ask of Mary love for those crosses made ready for us for all eternity, to lead us to bear them with more ease and perhaps with more merit.

"The Savior's body rests in the tomb; in three days it will rise again. Through the cross Jesus has won the greatest of all triumphs, the victory over sin and Satan, and He can say to his disciples: 'In the world you shall have distress: but have confidence, I have overcome the world.'"[4]

Virtue to be Prayed for -- Mercy

"Mercy," says St. Augustine, "is a heartfelt sympathy for another's distress, impelling us to help him if we can."

"It belongs to mercy to be generous to others and what is more to help others in their wants, which pertains chiefly to a superior. Hence, mercy is properly attributed to God and therein His all-powerfulness is said to be chiefly manifested. Of all the virtues which relate to our neighbor, mercy is the greatest, even as its act surpasses all others, since it belongs to one who is higher and better to supply the defect of another inasmuch as the latter is deficient.

"Although the sum total of the Christian religion consists in mercy, as regards external works; but the inward love of charity, whereby we are united to God takes precedence over both love and mercy for our neighbor. For charity likens us to God by uniting us to Him in the bond of love.

"Three things especially should inspire us to have mercy. First, its need, because he who does not show mercy will not find mercy. Secondly, its usefulness, because he who shows mercy will find mercy. Thirdly, its suitableness, because since we receive from all creatures, it is altogether fitting that we be merciful to others. For we are full of misery and unless persons showed mercy to us by giving themselves and favors to us we could not live. Therefore, it is sufficiently suitable that man since he needs mercy, should show mercy unto others."[5]

Teachings of Vatican II

"The Blessed Virgin advanced in her pilgrimage of faith and faithfully persevered in her union with her Son unto the cross, where she stood in keeping with the divine plan, grieving exceedingly with her only begotten Son, uniting herself with a maternal heart with His sacrifice, and lovingly consenting to the immolation of this Victim whom she herself had brought forth. Finally, she was given by the same Christ Jesus dying on a cross as a mother to His disciple with these words: 'Woman, behold thy son.'"[6]

Chapter 18

<u>*Glorious Mysteries*</u>

1. The Resurrection of Jesus

According to the Gospel of St. Matthew
(Chp. 28:1-10)

AFTER THE SABBATH, and towards dawn on the first day of the week, Mary of Magdala and the other Mary went to visit the sepulchre. And all at once there was a violent earthquake, for the angel of the Lord, descending from heaven, came and rolled away the stone and sat on it. His face was like lightning, his robe white as snow. The guards were so shaken, so frightened of him, that they were like dead men. But the angel spoke; and he said to the women, "There is no need for you to be afraid. I know you are looking for Jesus, who was crucified. He is not here for he has risen, as he said he would. Come and see the place where he lay, then go quickly and tell his disciples, "He has risen from the dead and now he is going before you to Galilee; it is there you will see him. Now I have told you." Filled with awe and great joy the women came quickly away from the tomb and ran to tell the disciples.

And there, coming to meet them, was Jesus. "Greetings" he said. And the women came up to him and, falling down before him, clasped his feet. Then Jesus said to them, "Do not be afraid; go and tell my brothers that they must leave for Galilee; they will see me there."

John 20:19-29

In the evening of that same day, the first day of the week, the doors were closed in the room where the disciples were, for fear of the Jews. Jesus came and stood among them. He said to them, "Peace be with you," and showed them his hands and his side. The disciples were filled with joy when they saw the Lord, and he said to them again, "Peace be with you."

"As the Father sent me, so am I sending you." After saying this he breathed on them and said: "Receive the Holy Spirit. For those whose sins you forgive, they are forgiven; for those whose sins you retain, they are retained."

Thomas, called the Twin, who was one of the Twelve, was not with them when Jesus came. When the disciples said, "We have seen the Lord," he answered, "Unless I see the holes that the nails made in his hands and can put my finger into the holes they made, and unless I can put my hand into his side, I refuse to believe." Eight days later the disciples were in the house again and Thomas was with them. The doors were closed, but Jesus came in and stood among them. "Peace be with you" he said. Then he spoke to Thomas, "Put your finger here; look, here are my hands. Give me your hand; put it into my side. Doubt no longer but believe." Thomas replied, "My Lord and my God!" Jesus said to him:

"You believe because you can see me. Happy are those who have not seen and yet believe."

Consideration of the Resurrection

"From the descent of Christ into limbo, we can gather four things.

"First of all, a firm hope in God should be enkindled in our hearts. For whenever we are suffering from trials and afflictions we should always hope in God for help, and confide in Him at all times. If Christ liberated those souls who were in limbo, by so much the more should he liberate each one of us if we are the friends of God, so that through Him we might be liberated from every evil and affliction.

On March 26, 2000, John Paul II prays in the Sepulcher
and kisses the marble slab covering the rock
where Jesus' body was laid.

The Chapel of the Primacy (JN 21: 15-19),
where Jesus told St. Peter to "feed my sheep," is located
in Tabgha, along the Sea of Galilee.

*John Paul II sitting in the Chapel of the Primacy
on March 24, 2000.*

"Secondly, we ought to entertain filial fear and rid ourselves of presumption. For although Christ suffered for sinners and descended into hell, still he did not set free all, but only those who were without mortal sin.

"Thirdly, an example of love comes to us from Christ's descent into limbo. For Christ descended into limbo to set free His own loyal friends, and consequently we should help the souls in purgatory. For the suffering souls in purgatory are powerless to help themselves and therefore we should from charity help them. We can assist the suffering souls by our Masses, prayers, and alms-giving."[1]

"It was necessary for Christ to rise again. First of all for the commendation of divine justice, to which it belongs to exalt them, who humble themselves for God's sake. Consequently, because Christ humbled Himself even to death on the cross, from love and obedience to God, it behooved Him to be uplifted by God to a glorious resurrection. Secondly, for our instruction in the faith, since our belief in Christ's Godhead is confirmed by His rising again. Thirdly, it was necessary for Christ to rise from the grave for the raising of our hope, since through seeing Christ who is our head, rise again, we hope that we likewise shall rise again. Fourthly, Christ arose from the dead to complete the work of our salvation, because just as for this reason did He endure evil, so was He glorified in rising in order to advance us toward good things."[2]

"It was becoming for Christ's soul at His Resurrection to resume the body with its scars. In the first place, for Christ's own glory. For St. Bede says that Christ kept His scars not from inability to heal them but to wear them as an everlasting trophy of His victory. Secondly, Christ rose with the scars on His body to confirm the hearts of His disciples as to the faith in His resurrection. Thirdly, that when He pleads for us with the Father, He may always show the manner of death He endured for us. Fourthly, that He may convince those redeemed in His blood how mercifully they have been helped, as He shows them the traces of the same death. Fifthly, Christ arose with the scars on His body so that on Judgment Day He might condemn the wicked with their just condemnation."[3]

"When the doors were shut, where the disciples were gathered together, for fear of the Jews, Jesus came and stood in the midst of them and said: 'Peace be to you' (Jn. 20:19). St. Augustine says: 'Certainly He was able to enter when the doors were shut, who at His birth preserved the virginity of His mother—inviolate.' Therefore, just as His Birth from His Virgin Mother was miraculous by the power of His Divinity, so was this entrance into the midst of His disciples miraculous. Jesus came and stood in the midst of the disciples. He Himself came personally, just as He had promised them. He stood in their midst, through courtesy and condescension; for He lived with them as one of them. And likewise to point out to us that we should be in the midst of virtue. And said: 'Peace be to you.' This salutation was necessary, for their peace was disturbed in many ways, first in regard to God; secondly, in regard to themselves; thirdly, in regard to the Jews. In regard to God, against whom they had sinned, some by denying Him, others by flight from Him. 'All you shall be scandalized in Me this night. For it is written: I will strike the Shepherd and the sheep of the flock shall be dispersed' (Mt. 26:31). And against this trial Jesus proposed to them the peace of reconciliation with God.

Likewise their peace was disturbed in regard to themselves, for they were sad and weak in faith; and hence Christ spoke peace to them. Likewise their peace was disturbed by persecutions from the Jews and in opposition to these persecutions and fears, Jesus said to His disciples: 'Peace be to you' (Jn. 20)."[4]

Fruit to be Prayed for -- The Peace of Christ

"Peace is nothing more than a tranquility of order. Man is said to be peaceful when the order of peace is threefold. First in regard to himself, secondly in regard to his God, and thirdly in regard to his neighbor.

It has been noted that in us three things should be regulated to obtain peace, namely: the intellect, the will, and the sensitive appetite, so that the will might be directed according to the mind. Here in this life we can possess this peace but imperfectly, because we are not entirely free from disturbance by other people, never wholly free from the snares of our enemies, the disturbers of our peace of mind. But in the kingdom of God we will enjoy perfect peace, for there our enemies cannot disturb us.

Christ, the Prince of Peace, said: 'My peace I give unto you, not as the world giveth do I give unto you.' Thus Christ distinguishes His peace from worldly peace. First, the peace of the world is ordained to the quiet and peaceful enjoyment of temporal things, and some-times sin and crime cooperate with the enjoyment of these things. But the peace of the Saints is ordained to eternal things.

Secondly, the peace of the world is a pretended or external peace. The nations are talking peace, but secretly and actively preparing for war. On the contrary, the peace Christ gives is true peace, both interiorly and exteriorly.

Third, the peace of the world is imperfect and fleeting, since it is for the quiet of the exterior man and not for the interior man. But the peace of Christ calms us interiorly and exteriorly."[5]

Teachings of John Paul II

"It is Christ who taught us that man is God's temple and that God's Spirit dwells in him. The great servant of Yahweh allowed the temple of His body to be destroyed, to be emptied to the point of death, because He had faith in the day of the Lord, the day when the Father in the power of the Spirit would rebuild the temple of His body."[6]

Catechism of the Catholic Church

"The empty tomb and the linen cloths lying there signify in them-selves that by God's power Christ's body had escaped the bonds of death and corruption. They prepared the disciples to encounter the Risen Lord (No. 657). Christ, "the first-born from the dead" (Col. 1:18), is the principle of our own resurrection, even now by the jus-tification of our souls (cf. Rom 6:4), and one day by the new life he will impart to our bodies" (cf. Rom 8:11) (No. 658).

Chapter 19

2. The Ascension of Jesus into Heaven

According to the Gospel of St. Matthew
(Chp. 28:16-20)

NOW THE ELEVEN disciples went to Galilee, to the mountain to which Jesus had directed them. And when they saw him they worshipped him; but some doubted. And Jesus came and said to them, "All authority in heaven and on earth has been given to me. Go therefore and make disciples of all nations, baptizing them in the name of the Father and of the Son and of the Holy Spirit, teaching them to observe all that I have commanded you; and lo, I am with you always, to the close of the age."

Acts of the Apostles 1:3-14

When he had been at table with them, he had told them not to leave Jerusalem, but to wait there for what the Father had promised. "It is," he had said, "what you have heard me speak about: John baptized with water but you, not many days from now, will be baptized with the Holy Spirit."

They asked him, "Lord, has the time come? Are you going to restore the kingdom to Israel?" He replied, "It is not for you to know times or dates that the Father has decided by his own authority, but you will receive power when the Holy Spirit comes on you, and then you will be my witnesses not only in Jerusalem but throughout Judea and Samaria, and indeed to the ends of the earth."

As he said this he was lifted up while they looked on, and a cloud took him from their sight. They were still staring into the sky when suddenly two men in white were standing near them and they said, "Why are you men from Galilee standing here looking into the sky? Jesus who has been taken up from you into heaven, this same Jesus will come back in the same way as you have seen him go there."

So from the Mount of Olives, as it is called, they went back to Jerusalem, a short distance away, no more than a Sabbath walk; and when they reached the city they went to the upper room where they were staying; there were Peter and John, James and Andrew, Philip and Thomas, Bartholomew and Matthew, James son of Alphaeus, and Simon the Zealot, and Jude son of James. All these joined in continuous prayer, together with several women, including Mary the Mother of Jesus, and with his brothers.

Consideration of the Ascension

"1. Christ was exalted on high, because He ascended into heaven.

"First of all, He ascended above all the terrestrial heavens. And Christ was the first to ascend into heaven.

"Secondly, He ascended above all the spiritual heavens, namely above all things of a spiritual nature.

"Thirdly, Christ ascended to the throne of His Father. 'God sitteth at the right hand of the Father,' means Our Lord's equality with the Father in the possession of spiritual goods.

"2. The Ascension of Christ was reasonable, because it took place in Heaven.

"First of all, because heaven was due to Christ from His very nature. For it is only natural that a thing return to the place whence it received its origin. But the principle of Christ's origin is from God, who is above all things. Secondly, heaven belonged to Christ, was owed to Him because of His victory. For Christ was sent into the world to fight against the devil and to conquer him, and therefore He merited to be exalted above all things.

"Thirdly, heaven was due to Christ by reason of His humility. For no humility is so great as the humility of Christ. He who is our Lord and Master willed to assume the form of a servant. For humility is the royal road to exaltation.

"3. The Ascension of Christ is useful to us, especially in regard to three things, namely, in regard to leadership, security, and the winning of our love.

"First, in regard to leadership. For Christ ascended into heaven to lead us there; for we did not know the way, but He has shown it to us, and He ascended so that he might make us secure in the possession of the heavenly kingdom.

"Secondly, in regard to our security. He likewise ascended for this purpose, that He might plead for us with the Father and render us eternally safe.

"Thirdly, He ascended so that He might win our hearts to Himself, 'Where thy treasure is there is thy heart also,' (Mt. 6:21) and so that we might despise temporal possessions. 'If you be risen with Christ, seek the things which are above, not the things. . . upon the earth,' (Col.3:1)."[1]

"4. Christ's Ascension is the cause of our salvation in two ways. First of all, on our part; secondly, on His.

"On our part, in so far as by the Ascension our souls are uplifted to Him: For His Ascension fosters, first, faith; secondly, hope; thirdly, charity.

"On His part, in regard to those things which, in ascending He did for our salvation.

"First, He prepared the way for our ascent into heaven according to His own words, 'I go to prepare a place for you.' (Jn. 14:2)

"Secondly, Christ entered heaven, to make intercession for us.

"Thirdly, that being established on His heavenly throne as God and Lord, He might send down gifts upon men, according to Eph. 4:10.

'He ascended above all the heavens, that He might fill all things,' that is fill all things with His gifts."[2]

Virtue to be Prayed for -- Hope

"The proper object of hope is eternal happiness. Hope reaches God by leaning on His help in order to obtain the desired good. Such a good is eternal life, which consists in the enjoyment of God Himself. For we should hope from Him for nothing less than Himself since His goodness, whereby He imparts good things to His creatures, is no less than His essence.

"Hope makes man adhere to God as to a principle wherefrom certain things come to us. Hope makes us adhere to God as the source from whence we derive perfect goodness, that is, by hope we trust in the Divine assistance for obtaining happiness.

"Hope has certainty, for hope is a certain expectation of future happiness. In this life we cannot know with certainty that we have grace. But hope does not trust chiefly on grace already received but on God's all-powerfulness and mercy, whereby even he that has not grace can obtain it, so as to come to eternal life.

"That some who have hope fail to obtain happiness is due to a fault of the free will in placing the obstacle of sin, but not any deficiency in God's power or mercy in which hope places its trust. Hence this does not prejudice the certainty of hope."[3]

Catechism of the Catholic Church

"Christ's ascension marks the definitive entrance of Jesus' humanity into God's heavenly domain, whence he will come again (cf Acts 1:11); this humanity in the meantime hides him from the eyes of men (cf Col 3:3) (No. 665). Jesus Christ, head of the Church, precedes us into the Father's glorious kingdom so that we, the members of his body, may live in the hope of one day being with him forever" (No. 666).

Chapter 20

3. The Descent of the Holy Spirit

According to the Acts of the Apostles
(Chp. 2: 1-17)

WHEN PENTECOST DAY came around, they had all met in one room, when suddenly they heard what sounded like a powerful wind from heaven, the noise of which filled the entire house in which they were sitting; and something appeared to them that seemed like tongues of fire; these separated and came to rest on the head of each of them. They were all filled with the Holy Spirit, and began to speak foreign languages as the Spirit gave them the gift of speech.

Now there were devout men living in Jerusalem from every nation under heaven, and at this sound they all assembled, each one bewildered to hear these men speaking his own language. They were amazed and astonished. "Surely," they said, "all these men speaking are Galileans? How does it happen that each of us hears them in his own native language? We hear them preaching in our own language about the marvels of God." Everyone was amazed and unable to explain it; they asked one another what it all meant. Some, however, laughed it off. "They have been drinking too much new wine" they said.

The Peter stood up with the eleven and addressed them in a loud voice: "Men of Judea, and all you who live in Jerusalem, make no mistake about this, but listen carefully to what I say. These men are not drunk as you imagine; why, it is only the third hour of the day. On the contrary, this is what the prophet spoke of: In the days to come—it is the Lord who speaks—I will pour out my spirit on all mankind. Their sons and daughters shall prophesy, your young men shall see visions, your old men shall dream dreams."

Chp. 2:32-33

God raised this man Jesus to life, and all of us are witnesses to that. Now raised to the heights by God's right hand, he has received from the Father the Holy Spirit, who was promised, and what you see and hear is the outpouring of that Spirit.

Chp. 2:36-41

"For this reason the whole House of Israel can be certain that God has made this Jesus whom you crucified both Lord and Christ." Hearing this, they were cut to the heart and said to Peter and the Apostles, "What must we do, brothers?" "You must repent," Peter answered "and everyone of you must be baptized in the name of Jesus Christ for the forgiveness of your sins, and you will receive the gift of the Holy Spirit. The promise that was made is for you and your children, and for all those who are far away, for all those whom the Lord our God will call to himself. He spoke to them for a long time using many arguments, and he urged them, "Save yourselves from this perverse generation." They were convinced by his arguments, and they accepted what he said and were baptized. That very day about three thousand were added to their number.

Consideration of the Descent of the Holy Spirit

"Amongst the disciples of our Lord, a twofold preparation was

The "Upper Room" of the Cenacle, where the event of Pentecost took place, is also the spot where Jesus instituted the priesthood and the Eucharist. He also appeared to the Apostles here after His Resurrection.

necessary, namely, pure love of the heart and obedience in action. Therefore, these two things, love and obedience, prepared them for the reception of the Holy Spirit. For since the Holy Spirit is love, He is given only to those who love God. For no one can truly love God, unless he has the Holy Spirit abiding in his soul, for we do not come to God before the grace of God, but it comes to us first."[1]

"The Holy Spirit is the Paraclete for He consoles us, when sadness arising from worldly disturbances afflicts us. He consoles us, in so far as He is the Love, which causes us to love God, and to have Him for our greatest friend. Because of the strength and consolation received from the Holy Spirit, 'the Apostles went forth from the presence of the council, rejoicing that they were accounted worthy to suffer reproach for the name of Jesus.'

"For just as the effect of the mission of the Son was to lead mankind to the Father, so the effect of the Holy Spirit is to lead the faithful to the Son.

"It is proper to a Divine Person to be a 'gift,' and to be given. But the Holy Spirit receives this proper name from the fact that He proceeds from the Father and Son. Therefore, 'gift,' is a name proper to the Holy Spirit. It is proper to the Holy Spirit to be given as God's gift to us, because of two reasons. First, because of the love by which God loves us, for one is said to give his love to another when one begins to love another. Secondly, because of the love with which we love God, because the Holy Spirit causes this love in us."[2]

"The blessings that come to us from the Holy Spirit are manifold and great.

"First, the Holy Spirit washes away our sins. The reason for this is, because it is the work of the Holy Spirit to renew and sanctify, as it is His work to establish us in the friendship of God. It is not surprising that the Holy Spirit purges sin, for all sins are removed—forgiven—through love. 'Many sins are forgiven thee, because thou has loved much,' said Christ to the repentant Magdalen.

"Secondly, the Holy Spirit enlightens our intellects, because all things which we know, we learn from the Holy Spirit. 'But the

Paraclete, the Holy Spirit, whom the Father will send in My Name, He will teach you all things and bring all things to your mind, whatsoever I will have said to you' (Jn. 14:26).

"Thirdly, the Holy Spirit aids us and encourages us to observe the commandments. For no one can keep the commandments of God, unless he loves God. "If any man love Me, he will keep My word" (Jn. 14:23). Therefore, the Holy Spirit causes us to love God.

"Fourthly, the Holy Spirit strengthens our hope in life everlasting, because He is as it were, the pledge of our eternal inheritance. "You were signed with the Holy Spirit, who is the pledge of our inheritance" (Eph. 1:13). For He is our safeguard to eternal life. The reason for this is, because eternal life is due man, inasmuch as the Son of God has won it for him, and He did this because man is like unto Christ. Now we become like unto Christ, when we have the Spirit of Christ—the Holy Spirit.

"Fifthly, the Holy Spirit counsels us concerning what is the will of God in regard to us. 'He that hath an ear, let him hear what the Spirit saith to the churches' (Apoc. 11:7)."[3]

The Fruits of this Mystery to be Prayed for -- The Gifts of the Holy Spirit

"Gifts are certain perfections of man by which he is disposed, so that he becomes promptly moved by divine inspiration, to act above a human manner and motives.

"First of all, things are understood from a simple truth. This is above the natural powers, and this takes place through the gift of understanding, for example when a man's mind is enlightened by faith from listening to the word of God.

"Secondly, the human mode of procedure in acquiring knowledge is this, that man from an inspection of the first principles and of the highest causes, judges and regulates concerning inferior things. And this happens through wisdom which is an intellectual gift. But when a man is united to these first causes (or First Cause), and transformed into their likeness, so that he clings to God with his whole soul; he then judges concerning the lowest things in their relation to the highest, and ordains not only things knowable, but also human conduct and passions in relation to God—(The First Cause). This mode of procedure is above the human way of doing things, and is accomplished by the gift of wisdom.

"Thirdly, on the part of man's actions, there ought to be counsel. In fact the human way is that which proceeds by inquiry and conjecture from those things which are accustomed to happen; but this mode of procedure is perfected by means of good counsel. But when a man accepts wholeheartedly what must be done, and is taught with certainty by the Holy Spirit, this is above the human way, and the gift of counsel does this very thing for us.

"Fourthly, on the part of the things done, the human way is, that from those things which are accustomed to happen often, man concerning new things, judges probably through counsel and furthermore, he places the order of this judgement on inferior things. But when a man knows with certainty those things which must occur, this is above man's power, and is achieved through the gift of knowledge.

"Inasmuch as the divine goodness is received from God and shines forth in God Himself, or from our neighbor, this is something above the human way, and is attributed to the gift of piety.

"Sixthly, when a man in all these things receives divine power or virtue, so that he exercises himself in the most difficult works of virtue, which exceed his own powers, and overcomes dangers which he could overcome only by divine help, this is also above the human way, and is accomplished by the gift of fortitude.

"Seventhly, inasmuch as man is attracted to temporal needful good, this is done through temperance. But when a man from a spirit of divine reverence considers all things as trash in comparison to God, this is something above the human way, and is perfected by the gift of filial fear."[4]

Teachings of Vatican II

"But since it has pleased God not to manifest solemnly the mystery of the salvation of the human race before He would pour forth the Spirit promised by Christ, we see the Apostles before the day of Pentecost 'persevering with one mind in prayer with the women and Mary the Mother of Jesus, and with His brethren,' and Mary by her prayers imploring the gift of the Spirit, who had already overshadowed her in the Annunciation."[5]

Teachings of John Paul II

"The present day Church seems to repeat with ever greater fervor and with holy insistence; 'Come, Holy Spirit!' Come! Come! 'Heal our wounds, our strength renew; On our dryness pour thy dew; Wash the stains of guilt away; Bend the stubborn heart and will; Melt the frozen, warm the chill; Guide the steps that go astray.' This appeal to the Spirit, intended to obtain the Spirit, is the answer to all the 'materialism' of our age."[6]

Catechism of the Catholic Church

"On the day of Pentecost when the seven weeks of Easter had come to an end, Christ's Passover is fulfilled in the outpouring of the Holy Spirit, manifested, given, and communicated as a divine person: of his fullness, Christ, the Lord, pours out the Spirit in abundance[122] (No. 731).

Chapter 21

4. The Assumption of Mary into Heaven

M ARY EXERCISED HER role of spiritual mother in the early Church after the Ascension of her Son. Three days after she died, Jesus assumed her into heaven, body and soul. Mary was immune from the consequences of original sin, so her body was incorrupt and taken up into heaven. She was seated next to her Son and there intercedes for her children, the Church, and all mankind. She intercedes as she did at the marriage feast of Cana where she said to her Son, "They have no wine." She said to the waiters, "Do whatever He tells you." Jesus yielded to a mother's prayer at "Cana of Galilee," and performed the miracle by which "His disciples believed in Him" (Author's Meditation).

Consideration of the Assumption of Mary

"1. I was exalted like a cedar in Libanus (Eccl. 25:17).

"The exaltation of Mary mentioned here can be understood as the six orders of the blessed by means of the six trees to which her exaltation is compared.

A cedar signifies patriarchs and prophets because of its natural loftiness.

A cypress signifies patriarchs and prophets because of its sweet odor.

A palm tree signifies the Apostles on account of their glorious victory over the world, for a palm is significant of triumph.

A rose signifies martyrs because of their effusion of blood which has a reddish color.

The elm tree signifies virgins for it grows by the river banks and is immune like virgins from the cold or heat of lustful desires.

The olive tree signifies confessors by reason of its oil.

"2. It is therefore in this sense that the Blessed Virgin is exalted as the Angels, patriarchs, prophets, Apostles, martyrs, confessors and virgins; even exalted above the choirs of Angels and all the Saints of heaven.

"She possessed the merit of a prophet by her prophecy 'Behold all generations shall call me Blessed' (Lk. 1). She saw with a prophetic vision and prophesied that she would be blessed by all nations, and that all nations must receive the Son of God, and her Son.

"She possessed the merit of the Apostles and Evangelists in teaching. For many things are written and preached which could not be known unless through her revelation, such as the visit of the Angel Gabriel to Mary and many other things.

"She possessed the merit of a martyr by patiently enduring the death of the cross with her Son. 'Thy own soul, a sword shall pierce' (Lk. 11).

"She possessed the merit of the confessors by devoutly acknowledging her Lord, 'My soul doth magnify the Lord' (Lk. 1).

"She possessed the merit of virgins in beginning and preserving her virginity. 'And the Angel Gabriel came to the Virgin Mary. (Lk. 1:27)"[1]

Fruit to be Prayed for --
Trust in Mary's Intercession

"The wine failing, the mother of Jesus said to Him: 'They have no wine' (Jn. 2:3).

"In Mary's intercession three things must be considered. First, her piety and mercy. For it pertains to mercy that a person has compassion for the defects or misery of another and regards them as one's own. Because the Blessed Virgin was full of mercy she wished to relieve the distress of others present at the marriage in Cana and hence she said to Jesus as the wine as failing, 'They have no wine.'

"Secondly, observe Mary's reverence for Christ. For from the reverence we have for God it is enough for us just to mention our defects or needs to Him. Therefore, His Blessed Mother simply mentioned the needs of the other guests saying, 'They have no wine.'

"Thirdly, observe the solicitude and diligence of the Virgin Mary. She did not wait to mention the needs until extreme necessity demanded but, 'as the wine was failing,' she took occasion to mention the fact to her Divine Son to relieve the marriage guests from an evident embarrassment."[2]

Teachings of Vatican II

"Taken up to heaven she did not lay aside this salvific duty, but by her constant intercession continued to bring us the gifts of eternal salvation. By her maternal charity, she cares for the brethren of her Son, who still journey on earth surrounded by dangers and difficulties, until they are led into the happiness of their true home."[3]

Teachings of John Paul II

"No matter how much the world may weigh upon us, no matter how much evil, sin, and suffering it may hold, the gaze of faith, fixed on the Mother of God, always discovers in her the 'dawn of a better world.' This is the special fruit of the feast of Mary's Assumption into heaven."[4]

Catechism of the Catholic Church

"Finally the Immaculate Virgin, preserved free from all stain of original sin, when the course of her earthly life was finished, was taken up body and soul into heavenly glory, and exalted by the Lord as Queen over all things, so that she might be the more fully conformed to her Son, the Lord of lords and conqueror of sin and death"[508] (No. 966).

Chapter 22

5. The Coronation of Mary

G OD THE FATHER crowned Mary, Queen of Heaven and Earth, and communicated to His daughter a share of His power. God the Son crowned Mary, His mother, and communicated to her a share of His wisdom. God the Holy Spirit crowned His spouse and communicated to her a share of His love. Mary is honored by the angels and saints as Queen of all the Universe and they serve her as their Queen. We, her children, honor Mary as our Queen and are moved to a filial love toward Mary and to the imitation of her virtues. (Author's Meditation).

Consideration of the Coronation of Mary as Queen of Heaven and Earth

"As we can form no idea of the final plenitude of charity which her holy soul possessed at the hour of death, neither can we determine the corresponding brilliance of the light of glory which she received nor the intensity of her vision into the most holy depths of the divine essence. She is queen of angels, of patriarchs, of prophets, of apostles, of martyrs, of confessors, of virgins, and of all saints, but she ever remains more our mother than our queen.[1]

Fruit to be Prayed for --
Grace of the Present Moment

"Let us keep asking Mary continually until death for the grace of the present moment. This is the grace that we beg of her when we pray, 'Holy Mary, Mother of God, pray for us now.' We plead for this most particular grace, which changes with each moment, makes us equal to the duties of the whole day, and opens our minds to the greatness of all those small things that bear a relationship to eternity. Let us ask for the grace to live to the full the richness of the passing moment, especially the time of prayer.

"Let us abandon to God's infinite mercy everything in our past and in our future and live practically and sublimely in the present moment, seeing in this fleeting now, whether it be dull or joyful or full of pain, a distant image of the unique instant of changeless eternity and, because of the actual grace which it contains, a living proof of God's fatherly goodness."[2]

Teachings of John Paul II

"Mary, in dependence on Christ, is the queen who possesses and exercise over the universe a sovereignty granted to her by her Son. Her queenship remains a corollary of her particular maternal mission and simply expresses the power conferred on her to carry out that mission. Mary's glorious state brings about a continuous and caring closeness. She knows everything that happens in our life and supports us with maternal love in life's trials."[3]

Chapter 23

Commentary on the Our Father and Hail Mary

S T. LOUIS DE Montfort wrote that "all our desires and all our needs are found expressed in these two prayers."[1]

"The Our Father has great value—above all because of its author who is the King of angels and men, Our Lord and Savior Jesus Christ. The Our Father contains all the duties we owe to God, the acts of all the virtues and the petitions for all our spiritual and corporal needs.

"St. John Chrysostom says that we cannot be our Master's disciples unless we pray as He did and in the way that He showed us. St. Augustine says that whenever we say the Our Father devoutly our venial sins are forgiven."[2]

The *Catechism of the Catholic Church* describes the Our Father as "truly the summary of the whole gospel."[3] It cites a passage from St. Thomas Aquinas on the Our Father: "The Lord's Prayer is the most perfect of prayers. In it we ask, not only for all the things we can rightly desire, but also in the sequence that they should be desired. This prayer not only teaches us to ask for things, but also in what order we should desire them."[4]

"The Hail Mary is a most concise summary of all that Catholic theology teaches about the Blessed Virgin. It is divided into two parts, that of praise and petition: the first shows all that goes to make up Mary's greatness and the second all that we need to ask her for and all that we may expect through her goodness."[5]

The wisdom of St. Louis de Montfort comes through in the following: "The Hail Mary is a blessed dew that falls from heaven upon the souls of the predestinate. It gives them a marvelous spiritual fertility so that they can grow in all virtues. The more the garden of the soul is watered by this prayer, the more enlightened one's intellect becomes, the more zealous his heart, and the stronger his armor against his spiritual enemies. The Hail Mary is a sharp and flaming shaft which, joined to the Word of God, gives the preacher the strength to pierce, move and convert the most hardened hearts even if he has little or no natural gift for preaching. This was the great secret that Our Lady taught St. Dominic and Alan de la Roche so that they might convert heretics and sinners. St. Antoninus tells us that this is why many priests got into the habit of saying a Hail Mary at the beginning of their sermons."[6]

In the book *True Devotion to Mary*, St. Louis de Montfort wrote: "Just as the salvation of the world began with the Hail Mary, so the salvation of each individual is bound up with it."[7] St. Louis also wrote in this excellent book, one which so shaped Pope John Paul II's devotion to Mary:" The Hail Mary is dew falling from heaven to make the soul fruitful. It is a pure kiss of love we give to Mary."[8]

In regards to the Hail Mary, St. Louis wrote: "It is the most perfect compliment you can offer to Mary, because it is the compliment which the Most High God Himself made to her, through an Archangel. It is by this compliment too, that you will infallibly gain her heart; if you recite the Hail Mary with proper devotion."[9]

As far as dryness in prayer goes, this is what St. Therese of the Child Jesus said: "When my state of spiritual aridity is such that not a single good thought will come, I repeat very slowly, the 'Our Father' and the 'Hail Mary,' which suffice to console me, and provide divine food for my soul."[10]

During Lent of 1274, St. Thomas Aquinas gave the following summary of the Our Father to students and townsfolk of Naples, Italy:

"By way of brief summary, it should be known that the Lord's

Prayer contains all that we ought to desire and all that we ought to avoid. Now, of all desirable things, that must be most desired which is most loved, and that is God.

"Therefore, you seek, first of all, the glory of God when you say: 'Hallowed be Thy name.' You should desire three things from God, and they concern yourself. The first is that you may arrive at eternal life. And you pray for this when you say: 'Thy kingdom come.' The second is that you will do the will of God and His justice. You pray for this in the words: 'Thy will be done on earth as it is in heaven.' The third is that you may have the necessaties of life. And thus you pray: 'Give us this day our daily bread.' Concerning all these things the Lord says: 'Seek ye first the kingdom of God,' which complies with the second, 'and all these things shall be added unto you' (Mt. 6:33), as in accord with the third.

"We must avoid and flee from all things which are opposed to the good. For, as we have seen, good is above all things to be desired. This good is fourfold. First, there is the glory of God, and no evil is contrary to this: 'If thou sin, what shalt thou hurt Him? And if thou do justly, what shall thou give Him?' (Job 35:6-7). Whether it be the evil inasmuch as God punishes it, or whether it be the good in that God rewards it—all redound to His glory.

"The second good is eternal life, to which sin is contrary: because eternal life is lost by sin. And so to remove this evil we pray: 'Forgive us our trespasses as we forgive those who trespass against us.' The third good is justice and good works, and temptation is contrary to this, because temptation hinders us from doing good. We pray, therefore, to have this evil taken away in the words: 'Lead us not into temptation.' The fourth good is all the necessaries of life, and opposed to this are troubles and adversities. And we seek to remove them when we pray: 'But deliver us from evil. Amen.'[11]

St. Thomas gave the following commentary to students and townsfolk on the first part of the Hail Mary during Lent, 1274 in Naples, Italy. (This commentary is from the Catechetical Instructions of St. Thomas Aquinas.)

"This salutation has three parts. The Angel gave one part, namely: 'Hail, full of grace, the Lord is with thee, blessed art thou among women' (Lk. 1:28). The other part was given by Elizabeth, the mother of John the Baptist, namely: 'Blessed is the fruit of they womb' (Lk. 1:42). The Church adds the third part, that is, 'Mary,' because the Angel did not say, 'Hail, Mary,' but 'Hail, full of grace.' But, as we shall see, this name, 'Mary,' according to its meaning agrees with the words of the Angels.

'Hail Mary'

"We must now consider concerning the first part of this prayer that in ancient times it was no small event when Angels appeared to men; and that man should show them reverence was especially praiseworthy. Thus, it is written to the praise of Abraham that he received the Angels with all courtesy and showed them reverence. But that an Angel should show reverence to a man was never heard of until the Angel reverently greeted the Blessed Virgin saying: 'Hail.'

The Angel's Dignity

"In olden times an Angel would not show reverence to a man, but a man would deeply revere an Angel. This is because Angels are greater than men, and indeed in three ways. First, they are greater than men in dignity. This is because the Angel is of a spiritual nature: 'Who makest Thy Angels spirits.' But, on the other hand, man is of a corruptible nature, for Abraham said: 'I will speak to my Lord, whereas I am dust and ashes.' It was not fitting, therefore, that a spiritual and incorruptible creature should show reverence to one that is corruptible as is a man. Secondly, an Angel is closer to God. The Angel, indeed, is of the family of God, and as it were stands ever by Him: 'Thousands of thousands ministered to Him, and ten thousand times a hundred thousand stood before Him.' Man, on the other hand, is rather a stranger and afar off from God because of sin: 'I have gone afar off.' Therefore, it is fitting that man should reverence an Angel who is an intimate and one of the household of the King.

"Then, thirdly, the Angels far exceed men in the fullness of the splendor of divine grace. For Angels participate in the highest degree in the divine light: 'Is there any numbering of His soldiers? And upon whom shall not His light arise? Hence, the angels always appear among men clothes in light, but men on the contrary, although they partake somewhat of the light of grace, nevertheless do so in a much slighter degree and with a certain obscurity. It was, therefore, not fitting that an Angel should show reverence to a man until it should come to pass that one would be found in human nature who exceeded the Angels in these three points in which we have seen that they excel over men—and this was the Blessed Virgin. To show that she excelled the Angels in these, the Angel desired to show her reverence, and so he said: '*Ave* (Hail).'

'Full of Grace'

"The Blessed Virgin was superior to any of the Angels in the fullness of grace, and as an indication of this the Angels showed reference to her by saying: 'Full of grace.' This is as if he said: 'I show thee reverence because thou dost excel me in the fullness of grace.'

The Blessed Virgin is said to be full of grace in three ways. First, as regards her soul, she was full of grace. The grace of God is given for two chief purposes, namely, to do good and to avoid evil. The Blessed Virgin, then, received grace in the most perfect degree, because she had avoided every sin more than any other saint after Christ. Thus it is said: 'Thou art all fair, My beloved, and there is not a spot in thee.' St. Augustine says: 'If we could bring together all the saints and ask them if they were entirely without sin, all of them, with the exception of the Blessed Virgin, would say with one voice: 'If we say that we have no sin, we deceive ourselves and the truth is not in us.' I except, however, this holy Virgin of whom, because of the honor of God, I wish to omit all mention of sin.' For we know that to her was granted grace to overcome every kind of sin by Him whom she merited to conceive and bring forth, and He certainly was wholly without sin.

Virtues of the Blessed Virgin

"She exercised the works of all the virtues, whereas the saints are conspicuous for the exercise of certain, special virtues. Thus, one excelled in humility, another in chastity, another in mercy, to the extent that they are the special exemplars of these virtues—as, for example, St. Nicholas is an exemplar of the virtue of mercy. The Blessed Virgin is the exemplar of all virtues.

"In her is the fullness of the virtue of humility: 'Behold the handmaid of the Lord.' And again: 'He hath regarded the humility of his handmaid.' So she is also exemplar of the virtue of chastity: 'Because I know not man.' And thus it is with all the virtues, as is evident. Mary was full of grace not only in the performance of all good, but also in the avoidance of all evil. Again, the Blessed Virgin was full of grace in the overflowing effect of this grace upon her flesh or body. For while it is a great thing in the saints that the abundance of grace sanctified their souls, yet, moreover, the soul of the holy Virgin was so filled with grace that from her soul grace poured into her flesh from which was conceived the Son of God. Hugh of St. Victor says of this: 'Because the love of the Holy Spirit so inflamed her soul, He worked a wonder in her flesh, in that from it was born God made Man.' 'And therefore also the Holy One which shall be born of thee shall be called the Son of God.'

Mary, Help of Christians

"The plenitude of grace in Mary was such that its effects overflow upon all men. It is a great thing in a saint when he has grace to bring about the salvation of many, but it is exceedingly wonderful when grace is of such abundance as to be sufficient for the salvation of all men in the world, and this is true of Christ and of the Blessed Virgin. Thus, 'a thousand bucklers,' that is, remedies against dangers, 'hang therefrom.' Likewise, in every work of virtue one can have her as one's helper. Of her it was spoken: 'In me is all grace of the way and of the truth, in me is all hope of life and of virtue.' Therefore, Mary is full of grace, exceeding the Angels in this fullness and very fittingly is she called, 'Mary' which means 'in herself enlightened': 'The Lord will fill thy soul with brightness.' And she will illumine others throughout the world, for which reason she is compared to the sun and to the moon.

'The Lord is With Thee'

"The Blessed Virgin excels the Angels in her closeness to God. The Angel Gabriel indicated this when he said: 'The Lord is with thee'—as if to say: 'I reverence thee because thou art nearer to God than I, because *the Lord is with thee.'* By the *Lord*, he means the Father with the Son and the Holy Spirit, who in like manner are not with any Angel or any other spirit; 'The Holy which shall be born of thee shall be called the Son of God.' God the Son was in her womb: 'Rejoice and praise, O thou habitation of Sion: for great is He that is in the midst of thee, the Holy One of Israel.'

"The Lord is not with the Angel in the same manner as with the Blessed Virgin; for with her He is as a Son, and with the Angel He is the Lord. The Lord, the Holy Spirit, is in her as in a temple, so that it is said: 'The temple of the Lord, the sanctuary of the Holy Spirit, because she conceived by the Holy Spirit. 'The Holy Spirit shall come upon thee.' The Blessed Virgin is closer to God than is an Angel, because with her are the Lord the Father, the Lord the Son, and the Lord the Holy Spirit—in a word, the Holy Trinity. Indeed of her we sing: 'Noble resting place of the Triune God.' 'The Lord is with thee' are the most praise-laden words that the Angel could have uttered; and, hence, he so profoundly reverenced the Blessed Virgin because she is the Mother of the Lord and Our Lady.

'Blessed art Thou among Women'

"The Blessed Virgin exceeds the Angels in purity. She is not only pure, but she obtains purity for others. She is purity itself, wholly lacking in every guilt of sin, for she never incurred either mortal or venial sin. So, too, she was free from the penalties of sin. Sinful man, on the contrary, incurs a threefold curse on account of sin. The first fell upon woman who conceives in corruption, bears her child with difficulty, and brings it forth in pain. The Blessed Virgin was wholly free from this, since she conceived without corruption, bore her Child in comfort, and brought Him forth in joy: 'It shall bud forth and blossom, and shall rejoice with joy and praise.'

"The second penalty was inflicted upon man in that he shall earn his bread by the sweat of his brow. The Blessed Virgin was also immune from this because, as the Apostle says, virgins are free from the cares of this world and are occupied wholly with the things of the Lord.'

"The third curse is common both to man and woman in that both shall one day return to dust. The Blessed Virgin was spared this penalty, for her body was raised up into heaven, and so we believe that after her death she was revived and transported into heaven: 'Arise, O Lord, into Thy resting place, Thou and the ark which Thou hast sanctified.' Because the Blessed Virgin was immune from these punishments, she is 'blessed among women.' Moreover, she alone escaped the curse of sin, brought forth the Source of blessing, and opened the gate of heaven. It is surely fitting that her name is 'Mary,' which is akin to the Star of the Sea (*Maria—maris stella*), for just as sailors are directed to port by the star of the sea, so also Christians are by Mary guided to glory.

'Blessed is the Fruit of Thy Womb'

"The sinner often seeks for something which he does not find; but to the just man it is given to find what he seeks: 'The substance of the sinner is kept for the just.' Thus, Eve sought the fruit of the tree (of good and evil), but she did not find in it that which she sought. Everything Eve desired, however, was given to the Blessed Virgin. Eve sought that which the devil falsely promised her, namely, that she and Adam would be as gods, knowing good and evil. 'You shall be,' says this liar, 'as gods.' But he lied, because 'he is a liar and the father of lies.' Eve was not made like God after having eaten the fruit, but rather she was unlike God in that by her sin she withdrew from God and was driven out of paradise. The Blessed Virgin, however, and all Christians found in the Fruit of her womb, Him, whereby we are all united to God and are made like to Him: 'When He shall appear, we shall be like to Him, because we shall see Him as He is.'

"Eve looked for pleasure in the fruit of the tree because it was good to eat. But she did not find this pleasure in it, and, on the contrary, she at once discovered she was naked and stricken with sorrow. In the Fruit of the Blessed Virgin we find sweetness and salvation: 'He that eateth My flesh . . . hath eternal life.'

"The fruit which Eve desired was beautiful to look upon, but the Fruit of the Blessed Virgin is far more beautiful, for the Angels desire to look upon Him: 'Thou art beautiful above the sons of men.' He is the splendor of the glory of the Father. Eve, therefore, looked in vain for that which she sought in the fruit of the tree, just as the sinner is disappointed in his sins. We must seek in the Fruit of the womb of the Virgin Mary whatsoever we desire. This is He who is the Fruit blessed by God, who has filled Him with every grace, which in turn is poured out upon us who adore Him: 'Blessed be God and the Father of our Lord Jesus Christ, who hath blessed us with spiritual blessings in Christ.' He, too, is revered by the Angels: 'Benediction and glory and wisdom and thanksgiving, honor and power and strength, to our God.' And He is glorified by men:

'Every tongue should confess that the Lord Jesus Christ is in the glory of God the Father.' The Blessed Virgin is indeed blessed, but far more blessed is the Fruit of her womb: 'Blessed is He who cometh in the name of the Lord.'"[12]

Chapter 24

Confraternity of the Holy Rosary

T HE CONFRATERNITY OF the Holy Rosary was originated by St. Dominic in the 13th century. Pope Leo XIII in his encyclical letter *Augustissimal Virginis*, Sept. 12, 1887 states: "For if we consider its origin, the Confraternity ranks first by reason of its antiquity, for its founding is attributed to St. Dominic himself." St. Louis de Montfort in his book *Secret of the Rosary* wrote: "As soon as St. Dominic acquainted Pope Innocent III with the fact that he had received a command from heaven to establish the Confraternity of the Holy Rosary, the Holy Father gave it his full approval, urged St. Dominic to preach it, and said he wished to become a member himself. Members of this Confraternity come from all walks of life: dukes, princes, as well as prelates, cardinals and Sovereign Pontiffs."[1] Regarding the Confraternity, St. Louis wrote: "The Blessed Virgin, protectress of the Church, has given us a most powerful means for appeasing her Son's anger, uprooting heresy and reforming Christian morals, in the Confraternity of the Rosary."[2]

The Confraternity retained its first fervor for 100 years after it was instituted by St. Dominic. After this, it was forgotten. Divine Providence assigned the restoration of the Confraternity of the Rosary in the 15th century to the eminent French Dominican theologian and preacher, Alan de la Roche. During his 16 years of teaching in France and Germany, he established himself as a renowned preacher of the

Rosary and Rosary Confraternity.

The Confraternity's first printed manual was written by the Dominican Jacob Sprenger and published in Cologne, Germany, in 1476. This manual stated that members needed to register their names and pray three Rosaries each week. Michael Francisci, a friend of Alan de la Roche, O.P., reported that by 1479, 500,000 people had registered their names and made the commitment to pray the three Rosaries each week that was expected of the members of the Confraternity.

In the 1560's, Turkish Moslem forces threatened Italy and Christian countries bordering the western Mediterranean Sea. Sultan Selim II stated his intention of taking the cross down from the top of St. Peter's in Rome and replacing it with a crescent. In 1569, the Dominican, Pope St. Pius V, enjoined the recitation of the Rosary on all Christendom for success in thwarting the advances of the Turkish Muslim forces. It was in this year that this great Pope of the Rosary wrote his apostolic letter *Consueverunt Romani Pontifices* which explained the power of the Rosary and how St. Dominic had devised this form of prayer and how he and his sons spread this form of prayer throughout the Church. He strongly encouraged people in this apostolic letter to enroll in the Confraternity of the Rosary. Pope Paul VI referred to this apostolic letter of St. Pius V in his apostolic exhortation, *Marialis Cultus*. He mentioned that in that document, Pope St. Pius V explained and in a certain sense established the traditional form of the Rosary.

In 1571, the Sultan and his armada of 300 ships huddled off the coast of Lepanto in a position to attack. Pope St. Pius V organized a papal fleet furnished by Venice, Genoa and Spain and led by Don Juan of Austria. This Marian Pope launched his own crusade of prayer, basing it on the Rosary. The great battle of Lepanto was fought. Processions of members of the Confraternity of the Rosary marched the streets of Rome and prayed for victory.

On October 7, 1571, Pope St. Pius V stood up at 4 o'clock in the afternoon during a conclave of cardinals and gazed out the window, then turning around to the cardinals, his face glowing with a strange light, announced: "This is no time for business. Go and thank God. Our fleet has just won the victory."[3] The papal treasurer, Bartolemeo Busotti, who was there reported the incident. Pope St. Pius V attributed the victory of Lepanto to the Rosaries of the Confraternity members. The Venetian Senate wrote to the other states which had taken part in the Crusade: *It was not generals nor battalions nor arms that brought us victory; but it was Our Lady of the Rosary.*

The Rosary Confraternity waned since the time of St. Louis de Montfort in the 18th century. This Rosary saint had been extremely active in encouraging people to enroll in the Confraternity of the Rosary. At the dawn of the 20th century, another great Pope of the Rosary appeared as the Supreme Pontiff. This was Pope Leo XIII who was instrumental in promoting the power and efficacy of the Rosary. He wrote extensively on the Rosary, more than any other Pope. During his twenty five years as Pope, he wrote twelve encyclicals on the Rosary, including one on the Confraternity of the Rosary.

This Pope of the Rosary constantly encouraged people to enroll in the Confraternity of the Rosary, an organization which he hoped would be helpful in strengthening the faithful in their journey of faith. In regards to the Confraternity, He wrote: "The end for which the Confraternity of the Rosary has been instituted is that many may be drawn to praise and honor the Blessed Virgin, and by unanimous supplication secure her patronage."

In 1893, Pope Leo XIII wrote an encyclical letter *Laetitiae Sanctae*, which he referred to members of the Confraternity as "the militant battalions who fight the battles of Christ by the power of His sacred mysteries under the banner and guidance of the Queen of Heaven. Mary had proven to them on every occasion and especially at Lepanto—how she accepted their prayers." As Leo XIII, at the dawn of the 20th century, held up the Rosary as the remedy for the evils of the time; so does John Paul II hold it up at the dawn of the 21st century. In November of 1980 in Fulda, Germany, he held up the

Rosary and said: "Here is the remedy against the evil."[4]

The Confraternity of the Rosary is a Spiritual Association. To become a member of the Confraternity, one must have their name inscribed in the register of membership wherever the Confraternity is canonically established. The only obligation (which does not bind under sin) imposed on the members of the Confraternity is to recite, during the course of each week, the 15 mysteries of the Rosary, while devoutly meditating on them. All members pray for one another and for the intentions of one another. The Order of St. Dominic admits all members of the Rosary Confraternity to share in the Masses, Rosaries, prayers, apostolic work and penances of all the Fathers, Brothers, Cloistered Nuns, Convents of Sisters and thousands of lay— Third Order members around the world.

Mary has promised in her well-known Rosary promises, "I have obtained from my Son that all members of the Confraternity of the Rosary shall have in life and in death all the Blessed in Heaven as their intercessors." Pope Leo XIII stated in the apostolic constitution *Ubi Primuni* the purpose, structure, works and organization of the Rosary Confraternity. In this apostolic constitution he wrote: "For whenever a person fulfills his obligation of reciting the Rosary according to the rule of the Confraternity, he includes in his intentions all its members, and they in turn render him service many times over."

Saint John Vianney said, "If anyone has the happiness of being in the Confraternity of the Holy Rosary, he and she have in all corners of the globe brothers and sisters who pray for them."

St. Louis de Montfort wrote: "Believe me, dear members of the Rosary Confraternity, if you genuinely wish to reach a high-level of prayer in all honesty and without falling into the traps that the devil sets for those who pray, say your whole Rosary everyday, or at least five decades of it."[5] Ecclesiastical writers have called the Confraternity of the Rosary "the praying army enrolled by St. Dominic under the banner of the Mother of God."[6]

"In his bull on the Rosary, Pope Gregory XIII says very clearly that the public prayers and processions of members of the Confraternity of the Holy Rosary were largely responsible for the great victory over the Turkish Navy at Lepanto which Almighty God granted to Christians on the first Sunday of October, 1571."[7]

The Dominican Alan de la Roche assured people of his time that the Holy Rosary "is the root and the storehouse of countless blessings. For through the Holy Rosary:

1. Sinners are forgiven.
2. Souls that thirst are refreshed.
3. Those who weep find happiness.
4. Those who are tempted find peace.
5. The poor find help.
6. Religious are reformed.
7. Those who are ignorant are instructed."

Since the days of St. Dominic, the Rosary has been the special charism of the Dominican Order. The Catholic Church looks to the Dominicans as official promoters of both the Rosary and Rosary Confraternity.

If you wish to be a member of the Confraternity of the Holy Rosary, send your full name and address to:

Rosary Center
Dominican Fathers
P.O. Box 3617
Portland, Oregon 97208

Conclusion

THE POPES HAVE BEEN the main teachers and guardians of the Rosary tradition. St. Dominic and his family, the Dominican Order, have been the main teachers of the Rosary devotion over the centuries. Many Popes have praised Mary's school, the Rosary, as a spiritual training school. Many saints enrolled in Mary's school, the Rosary, and greatly benefited from it. They encouraged others to pray the Rosary as a means of growing in holiness. In our times, the Rosary can help us to respond to Vatican II's "call to holiness."

Pope John Paul II is a true champion of the Rosary. He has continued the legacy of Leo XIII to all Popes succeeding him: to teach the Rosary. John Paul II sees the Rosary as a prayer we pray with Mary as the Apostles prayed with her in the Upper Room. He sees the Rosary as a means of meditating with Mary on the mysteries of her Son, which she, as Mother, pondered in her heart. At Fatima, Mary appeared as the Lady of the Rosary. Her message on each of the six apparitions was: "Pray the Rosary every day." When John Paul II went to Fatima in 1982, he said: "The Lady of the message points to the Rosary."

The Rosary is a "Gospel prayer" as Paul VI was to state. The soul of the Rosary is meditation on the 15 mysteries. Pope St. Pius V taught that meditation enlightens the mind and the spark from the enlightened mind sets the heart on fire.

It is hoped that the wisdom and teachings of the Church, the Popes and saints, especially St. Thomas Aquinas, has deepened the knowledge and prayer life of the readers. It is hoped that this book has helped to deepen our understanding and appreciation of the Rosary as a true and efficacious prayer in the life of the Church. As a spiritual treasure in the Church's devotional life, may the Rosary deepen our relationship with Jesus through Mary.

Appendix 1

Lumen Gentium: Chapter 8
The Blessed Virgin Mary, Mother of God in the Mystery of Christ and the Church

1. Introduction

52. Wishing in his supreme goodness and wisdom to effect the redemption of the world, "when the fullness of time came, God sent his Son, born of a woman...that we might receive the adoption of sons" (Gal. 4:4-5). "He for us men, and for our salvation, came down from heaven, and was incarnate by the Holy Spirit from the Virgin Mary."[1] This divine mystery of salvation is revealed to us and continued in the Church, which the Lord established as his body. Joined to Christ the head and in the unity of fellowship with all his saints, the faithful must in the first place reverence the memory "of the glorious ever Virgin Mary, Mother of our God and Lord Jesus Christ."[2]

53. The Virgin Mary, who at the message of the angel received the Word of God in her heart and in her body and gave Life to the world, is acknowledged and honored as being truly the Mother of God and Mother of the Redeemer. Redeemed by reason of the merits of her Son and united to him by a close and indissoluble tie, she is endowed with the high office and dignity of being the Mother of the Son of God, by which account she is also the beloved daughter of the Father and the temple of the Holy Spirit. Because of this gift of sublime grace she far surpasses all creatures, both in heaven and on earth. At the same time, however, because she belongs to the offspring of Adam she is one with all those who are to be saved. She is "the mother of the members of Christ...having cooperated by charity that faithful

might be born in the Church, who are members of that head."[3] Wherefore she is hailed as a preeminent and singular member of the Church,
and as its type and excellent exemplar in faith and charity. The Catholic Church, taught by the Holy Spirit, honors her with filial affection
and piety as a most beloved mother.

54. Wherefore this holy synod, in expounding the doctrine on the
Church, in which the divine Redeemer works salvation, intends to
describe with diligence both the role of the Blessed Virgin in the
mystery of the Incarnate Word and the Mystical Body, and the duties
of redeemed mankind toward the Mother of God, who is mother of
Christ and mother of men, particularly of the faithful. It does not,
however, have it in mind to give a complete doctrine on Mary, nor
does it wish to decide those questions which the work of theologians
has not yet fully clarified. Those opinions, therefore, may be law-
fully retained which are propounded in Catholic schools concerning
her, who occupies a place in the Church which is the highest after
Christ and yet very close to us.[4]

II. The Role of the Blessed Mother in the Economy of Salvation

55. The Sacred Scriptures of both the Old and the New Testament,
as well as ancient Tradition, show the role of the Mother of the Savior in the economy of salvation in an ever clearer light and draw
attention to it. The books of the Old Testament describe the history
of salvation, by which the coming of Christ into the world was slowly
prepared. These earliest documents, as they are read in the Church
and are understood in the light of a further and full revelation, bring
the figure of the woman, Mother of the Redeemer, into a gradually
clearer light. When it is looked at in this way, she is already pro-
phetically foreshadowed in the promise of victory over the serpent,
which was given to our first parents after their fall into sin (cf. Gen
3:15). Likewise she is the Virgin who shall conceive and bear a son,
whose name will be called Emmanuel (cf. Is 7:14; cf. Mi 5:2-3; Mt
1:22-23). She stands out among the poor and humble of the Lord,

who confidently hope for and receive salvation from him. With her, the exalted Daughter of Sion, and after a long expectation of the promise, the times are fulfilled and the new economy established, when the Son of God took a human nature from her, that he might in the mysteries of his flesh free man from sin.

56. The Father of mercies willed that the Incarnation should be preceded by the acceptance of her who was predestined to be the mother of his Son, so that just as a woman contributed to death, so also a woman should contribute to life. That is true in outstanding fashion of the mother of Jesus, who gave to the world him who is Life itself and who renews all things, and who was enriched by God with the gifts which befit such a role. It is no wonder therefore that the usage prevailed among the Fathers whereby they called the mother of God entirely holy and free from all stain of sin, as though fashioned by the Holy Spirit and formed as a new creature.[5] Adorned from the first instant of her conception with the radiance of an entirely unique holiness, the Virgin of Nazareth is greeted, on God's command, by an angel messenger as "full of grace" (cf. Lk 1:28), and to the heavenly messenger she replies: "Behold the handmaid of the Lord, be it done unto me according to thy word" (Lk 1:38). Thus Mary, a daughter of Adam, consenting to the divine Word, became the mother of Jesus, the one and only Mediator. Embracing God's salvific will with a full heart and impeded by no sin, she devoted herself totally as a handmaid of the Lord to the person and work of her Son, under him and with him, by the grace of almighty God, serving the mystery of redemption. Rightly, therefore the holy Fathers see her as used by God not merely in a passive way, but as freely cooperating in the work of human salvation through faith and obedience. For, as St. Irenaeus says, she "being obedient, became the cause of salvation for herself and for the whole human race."[6] Hence not a few of the early Fathers gladly assert in their preaching, "The knot of Eve's disobedience was untied by Mary's obedience; what the virgin Eve bound through her unbelief, the Virgin Mary loosened by her faith."[7] Comparing Mary with Eve, they call Mary

"the Mother of the living,"[8] and still more often they say: "death through Eve, life through Mary."[9]

57. This union of the Mother with the Son in the work of salvation is made manifest from the time of Christ's virginal conception up to his death. It is shown first of all when Mary, arising in haste to go to visit Elizabeth, is greeted by her as blessed because of her belief in the promise of salvation and the precursor leaped with joy in the womb of his mother (cf. Lk 1:41-45). This union is manifest also at the birth of our Lord, who did not diminish his mother's virginal integrity but sanctified it[10] when the Mother of God joyfully showed her firstborn Son to the shepherds and Magi. When she presented him to the Lord in the temple, making the offering of the poor, she heard Simeon foretelling at the same time that her Son would be a sign of contradiction and that a sword would pierce the mother's soul, that out of many hearts thoughts might be revealed (cf. Lk 2:34-35). When the child Jesus was lost and they had sought him sorrowing, his parents found him in the temple, taken up with the things that were his Father's business, and they did not understand the word of their Son. His Mother indeed kept these things to be pondered over in her heart (cf. Lk 2:41-51).

58. In the public life of Jesus, Mary makes significant appearances. This is so even at the very beginning, when at the marriage feast of Cana, moved with pity, she brought about by her intercession the beginning of miracles of Jesus the Messiah (cf. Jn 2:1-11). In the course of her Son's preaching she received the words whereby, in extolling a kingdom beyond the calculations and bonds of flesh and blood, he declared blessed (cf. Mk 3:35; par. Lk 11:27-28) those who heard and kept the Word of God, as she was faithfully doing (cf. Lk 2:19, 51). After this manner the Blessed Virgin advanced in her pilgrimage of faith, and faithfully persevered in her union with her Son unto the cross, where she stood, in keeping with the divine plan (cf. Jn 19:25), grieving exceedingly with her only begotten Son, uniting herself with a maternal heart with his sacrifice, and lovingly consenting to the immolation of this victim which she herself had brought

forth. Finally, she was given by the same Christ Jesus dying on the cross as a mother to his disciple with these words: "Woman, behold thy son"[11] (cf. Jn 19:26-27).

59. But since it has pleased God not to manifest solemnly the mystery of the salvation of the human race before he would pour forth the Spirit promised by Christ, we see the apostles before the day of Pentecost "persevering with one mind in prayer with the women and Mary, the Mother of Jesus, and with his brethren" (Acts 1:14), and Mary by her prayers imploring the gift of the Spirit, who had already overshadowed her in the annunciation. Finally, the Immaculate Virgin, preserved free from all guilt of original sin,[12] on the completion of her earthly sojourn was taken up by body and soul into heavenly glory[13] and exalted by the Lord as queen of the universe, that she might be the more fully conformed to her Son, the Lord of lords (cf. Rv 19:16) and the conqueror of sin and death.[14]

III. On the Blessed Virgin and the Church

60. There is but one Mediator, as we know from the words of the Apostle, "for there is one God and one mediator of God and men, the man Christ Jesus, who gave himself a redemption for all" (1 Tm 2:5-6). The maternal duty of Mary toward men in no wise obscures or diminishes this unique mediation of Christ, but rather shows his power. For all the salvific influence of the Blessed Virgin on men originates, not from some inner necessity, but from the divine pleasure. It flows forth from the superabundance of the merits of Christ, rests on his mediation, depends entirely on it and draws all its power from it. In no way does it impede, but rather does it foster the immediate union of the faithful with Christ.

61. Predestined from eternity to be the Mother of God by that decree of divine providence which determined the Incarnation of the Word, the Blessed Virgin was on this earth the virgin Mother of the Redeemer, and above all others and in a singular way the generous associate and humble handmaid of the Lord. She conceived, brought

forth and nourished Christ. She presented him to the Father in the temple, and was united with him by compassion as he died on the cross. In this singular way she cooperated by her obedience, faith, hope and burning charity in the work of the Savior in giving back supernatural life to souls. Wherefore she is our mother in the order of grace.

62. This maternity of Mary in the order of grace began with the consent which she gave in faith at the annunciation and which she sustained without wavering beneath the cross, and lasts until the eternal fulfillment of all the elect. Taken up to heaven she did not lay aside this salvific duty, but by her constant intercession continued to bring us the gifts of eternal salvation.[15] By her maternal charity, she cares for the brethren of her Son, who still journey on earth surrounded by dangers and difficulties, until they are led into the happiness of their true home. Therefore the Blessed Virgin is invoked by the Church under the titles of Advocate, Auxiliatrix, Adjutrix and Mediatrix.[16] This, however, is to be so understood that it neither takes away from nor adds anything to the dignity and efficaciousness of Christ the one Mediator[17]

For no creature could ever be counted as equal with the incarnate Word and Redeemer. Just as the priesthood of Christ is shared in various ways both by the ministers and by the faithful, and as the one goodness of God is really communicated in different ways to his creatures, so also the unique mediation of the Redeemer does not exclude but rather gives rise to a manifold cooperation which is but a sharing in this one source.

The Church does not hesitate to profess this subordinate role of Mary. It knows it through unfailing experience of it and commends it to the hearts of the faithful, so that encouraged by this maternal help they may the more intimately adhere to the Mediator and Redeemer.

63. By reason of the gift and role of divine maternity, but which she is united with her Son, the Redeemer, and with his singular graces and functions, the Blessed Virgin is also intimately united with the

Church. As St. Ambrose taught, the Mother of God is a type of the Church in the order of faith, charity and perfect union with Christ.[18] For in the mystery of the Church, which is itself rightly called mother and virgin, the Blessed Virgin stands out in eminent and singular fashion as exemplar both of virgin and mother.[19] By her belief and obedience, not knowing man but overshadowed by the Holy Spirit, as the new Eve she brought forth on earth the very Son of the Father, showing an undefiled faith, not in the word of the ancient serpent, but in that of God's messenger. The Son whom she brought forth is he whom God placed as the first-born among many brethren (Rm 8:29), namely the faithful, in whose birth and education she cooperates with a maternal love.

64. The Church indeed, contemplating her hidden sanctity, imitating her charity and faithfully fulfilling the Father's will, by receiving the Word of God in faith becomes herself a mother. By her preaching she brings forth to a new and immortal life the sons who are born to her in baptism, conceived of the Holy Spirit and born of God. She herself is a virgin, who keeps whole and entire the faith given to her by her spouse. Imitating the mother of her Lord, and by the power of the Holy Spirit, she keeps with virginal purity an entire faith, a firm hope and a sincere charity.[20]

65. But while in the most holy Virgin the Church has already reached that perfection whereby she is without spot or wrinkle, the followers of Christ still strive to increase in holiness by conquering sin (cf. Eph 5:27). And so they turn their eyes to Mary, who shines forth to the whole community of the elect as the model of virtues. Piously meditating on her and contemplating her in the light of the Word made man, the Church with reverence enters more intimately into the great mystery of the Incarnation and becomes more and more like her spouse. For Mary, who since her entry into salvation history unites in herself and re-echoes the greatest teachings of the faith as she is proclaimed and venerated, calls the faithful to her Son and his sacrifice and to the love of the Father. Seeking after the glory of Christ, the Church becomes more like her exalted type, and continually

progresses in faith, hope and charity, seeking and doing the will of God in all things. Hence, the Church, in her apostolic work also, justly looks to her, who brought forth Christ, who was conceived of the Holy Spirit and born of the Virgin, that through the Church he may be born and may increase in the hearts of the faithful also. The Virgin in her own life lived an example of that maternal love, by which it behooves that all should be animated who cooperate in the apostolic mission of the Church for the regeneration of men.

IV. The Cult of the Blessed Virgin in the Church

66. Placed by the grace of God, as God's Mother, next to her Son and exalted above all angels and men, Mary intervened in the mysteries of Christ and is justly honored by a special cult in the Church. Clearly, from earliest times the Blessed Virgin is honored under the title of Mother of God, under whose protection the faithful took refuge in all their dangers and necessities.[21] Hence, after the Synod of Ephesus the cult of the People of God toward Mary wonderfully increased in veneration and love, in invocation and imitation, according to her own prophetic words: "All generations shall call me blessed, because he that is mighty hath done great things to me" (Lk 1:48). This cult, as it always existed, although it is altogether singular, differs essentially from the cult of adoration which is offered to the incarnate Word, as well to the Father and the Holy Spirit, and it is most favorable to it. The various forms of piety toward the Mother of God, which the Church, within the limits of sound and orthodox doctrine, according to the conditions of time and place, and the nature and ingenuity of the faithful, has approved, bring it about that while the Mother is honored, the Son, through whom all things have their being (cf. Col 1:15-16) and in whom it has pleased the Father that all fullness should dwell (Col 1:19), is rightly known, loved and glorified, and that all his commands are observed.

67. This most holy synod deliberately teaches this Catholic doctrine and at the same time admonishes all the sons of the Church that

the cult, especially the liturgical cult, of the Blessed Virgin be generously fostered, and the practices and exercises of piety, recommended by the magisterium of the Church toward her in the course of centuries, be made of great moment, and those decrees, which have been given in the early days regarding the cult of images of Christ, the Blessed Virgin and the saints, be religiously observed.[22] But it exhorts theologians and preachers of the divine Word to abstain zealously both from all gross exaggerations as well as from petty narrow-mindedness in considering the singular dignity of the Mother of God.[23] Following the study of Sacred Scripture, the holy Fathers, the doctors and liturgy of the Church, and under the guidance of the Church's magisterium, let them rightly illustrate the duties and privileges of the Blessed Virgin which always look to Christ, the source of all truth, sanctity and piety. Let them assiduously keep away from whatever, either by word or deed, could lead separated brethren or any other into error regarding the true doctrine of the Church. Let the faithful remember moreover that true devotion consists neither in sterile or transitory affection, nor in a certain vain credulity, but proceeds from true faith, by which we are led to know the excellence of the Mother of God, and we are moved to a filial love toward our mother and to the imitation of her virtues.

V. Mary the Sign of Created Hope
   and Solace to the Wandering People of God

68. In the interim, just as the Mother of Jesus, glorified in body and soul in heaven, is the image and beginning of the Church as it is to be perfected in the world to come, so too does she shine forth on earth, until the day of the Lord shall come (cf. 2 Pt 3:10), as a sign of sure hope and solace to the People of God during its sojourn on earth.

69. It gives great joy and comfort to this holy and general synod that even among the separated brethren there are some who give due honor to the Mother of our Lord and Savior, especially among the Orientals, who with devout mind and fervent impulse give honor to

the Mother of God, ever virgin.[24]   The entire body of the faithful pours forth urgent supplications to the Mother of God and Mother of men, that she, who aided the beginnings of the Church by her prayers, may now, exalted as she is above all the angels and saints, intercede before her Son in the fellowship of all the saints, until all families of people, whether they are honored with the title of Christian or whether they still do not know the Savior, may be happily gathered together in peace and harmony into one people of God, for the glory of the most holy and undivided Trinity.

Each and all of these items which are set forth in this dogmatic Constitution have met with the approval of the Council Fathers. And We by the apostolic power given Us by Christ, together with the venerable Fathers in the Holy Spirit, approve, decree and establish it and command that what has thus been decided in the Council be promulgated for the glory of God.

Given in Rome at St. Peter's on November 21, 1964

Appendix 2

Marialis Cultus: Part Three
The Rosary

42. We wish now, venerable Brothers, to dwell for a moment on the renewal of the pious practice which has been called "the compendium of the entire Gospel"[110]: the Rosary. To this our predecessors have devoted close attention and care. On many occasions they have recommended its frequent recitation, encouraged its diffusion, explained its nature, recognized its suitability for fostering contemplative prayer–prayer of both praise and petition–and recalled its intruistic effectiveness for promoting Christian life and apostolic commitment.

We, too, from the first general audience of our pontificate on July 13, 1963, have shown our great esteem for the pious practice of the Rosary.[111] Since that time we have underlined its value on many different occasions, some ordinary, some grave. Thus, at a moment of anguish and uncertainty, we published the Letter *Christi Matri* (September 15, 1966), in order to obtain prayers to Our Lady of the Rosary and to implore from God the supreme benefit of peace.[112] We renewed this appeal in our Apostolic Exhortation *Recurrens mensis October* (October 7, 1969), in which we also commemorated the fourth centenary of the Apostolic Letter *Consueverunt Romani pontifices* of our predecessor Saint Pius V, who in that document explained an in a certain sense established the traditional form of the Rosary.[113]

43. Our assiduous and affectionate interest in the Rosary has led us to follow very attentively the numerous meetings which in recent years have been devoted to the pastoral role of the Rosary in the

modern world, meetings arranged by associations and individuals profoundly attached to the Rosary and attended by bishops, priests, religious and lay people of proven experience and recognized ecclesial awareness. Among those people special mention should be made of the sons of Saint Dominic, by tradition the guardians and promoters of this very salutary practice. Parallel with such meetings has been the research work of historians, work aimed not at defining in a sort of archaeological fashion the primitive form of the Rosary but at uncovering the original inspiration and driving force behind it and its essential structure. The fundamental characteristics of the Rosary, its essential elements and their mutual relationship have all emerged more clearly from these congresses and from the research carried out.

44. Thus, for instance, the Gospel inspiration of the Rosary has appeared more clearly: the Rosary draws from the Gospel the presentation of the mysteries and its main formulas. As it moves from the angel's joyful greeting and the Virgin's pious assent, the Rosary takes its inspiration from the Gospel to suggest the attitude with which the faithful should recite it. In the harmonious succession of *Hail Mary's* the Rosary puts before us once more a fundamental mystery of the Gospel–the Incarnation of the Word, contemplated at the decisive moment of the Annunciation to Mary. The Rosary is thus a Gospel prayer, as pastors and scholars like to define it, more today perhaps than in the past.

45. It has also been more easily seen how the orderly and gradual unfolding of the Rosary reflects the very way in which the Word of God, mercifully entering into human affairs, brought about the Redemption. The Rosary considers in harmonious succession the principal salvific events accomplished in Christ, from His virginal conception and the mysteries of His childhood to the culminating moments of the Passover–the blessed passion and the glorious resurrection–and to the effects of this on the infant Church on the day of Pentecost, and on the Virgin Mary when at the end of her earthly life she was assumed body and soul into her heavenly home. It has also

been observed that the division of the mysteries of the Rosary into three parts not only adheres strictly to the chronological order of the facts but above all reflects the plan of the original proclamation of the Faith and sets forth once more the mystery of Christ in the very way in which it is seen by Saint Paul in the celebrated "hymn" of the Letter of the Philippians–kenosis, death and exaltation (cf. 2:6-11).

46. As a Gospel prayer, centered on the mystery of the redemptive Incarnation, the Rosary is therefore a prayer with a clearly Christological orientation. Its most characteristic element, in fact, the litany-like succession of *Hail Mary's*, becomes in itself an unceasing praise of Christ, who is the ultimate object both of the angel's announcement and of the greeting of the mother of John the Baptist: "Blessed is the fruit of your womb" (Lk. 1:42). We would go further and say that the succession of *Hail Mary's* constitutes the warp on which is woven the contemplation of the mysteries. The Jesus that each *Hail Mary* recalls is the same Jesus whom the succession of the mysteries proposes to us–now as the Son of God, now as the Son of the Virgin–at His birth in a stable at Bethlehem, at His presentation by His Mother in the Temple, as a youth full of zeal for His Father's affairs, as the Redeemer in agony in the garden, scourged and crowned with thorns, carrying the cross and dying on Calvary; risen from the dead and ascended to the glory of the Father to send forth the gift of the Spirit. As is well known, at one time there was a custom, still preserved in certain places, of adding to the name of Jesus in each *Hail Mary* a reference to the mystery being contemplated. And this was done precisely in order to help contemplation and to make the mind and the voice act in unison.

47. There has also been felt with greater urgency the need to point out once more the importance of a further essential element in the Rosary, in addition to the value of the elements of praise and petition, namely the element of contemplation. Without this the Rosary is a body without a soul, and its recitation is in danger of becoming a mechanical repetition of formulas and of going counter to the warning of Christ: "And in praying do not heap up empty phrases as the

Gentiles do; for they think that they will be heard for their many words" (Mt. 6:7). By its nature the recitation of the Rosary calls for a quiet rhythm and a lingering pace, helping the individual to meditate on the mysteries of the Lord's life as seen through the eyes of her who was closest to the Lord. In this way the unfathomable riches of these mysteries are unfolded.

48. Finally, as a result of modern reflection the relationships between the liturgy and the Rosary have been more clearly understood. On the one hand it has been emphasized that the Rosary is, as it were, a branch sprung from the ancient trunk of the Christian liturgy, the Psalter of the Blessed Virgin, whereby the humble were associated in the Church's hymn of praise and universal intercession. On the other hand it has been noted that this development occurred at a time–the last period of the Middle Ages–when the liturgical spirit was in decline and the faithful were turning from the liturgy towards a devotion to Christ's humanity and to the Blessed Virgin Mary, a devotion favoring a certain external sentiment of piety. Not many years ago some people began to express the desire to see the Rosary included among the rites of the liturgy, while other people, anxious to avoid repetition of former pastoral mistakes, unjustifiably disregarded the Rosary. Today the problem can easily be solved in the light of the principles of the Constitution *Sacrosanctum concilium*. Liturgical celebrations and the pious practice of the Rosary must be neither set in opposition to one another nor considered as being identical.[114] The more an expression of prayer preserves its own true nature and individual characteristics the more fruitful it becomes. Once the pre-eminent value of liturgical rites has been reaffirmed it will not be difficult to appreciate the fact that the Rosary is a practice of piety which easily harmonizes with the liturgy. In fact, like the liturgy, it is of a community nature, draws its inspiration from Sacred Scripture and is oriented towards the mystery of Christ. The commemoration in the liturgy and the contemplative remembrance proper to the Rosary, although existing on essentially different planes of reality, have as their object the same salvific events wrought by Christ.

The former presents anew, under the veil of signs and operative in a hidden way, the great mysteries of our Redemption. The latter, by means of devout contemplation, recalls these same mysteries to the mind of the person praying and stimulates the will to draw from them the norms of living. Once this substantial difference has been established, it is not difficult to understand that the Rosary is an exercise of piety that draws its motivating force from the liturgy and leads naturally back to it, if practiced in conformity with its original inspiration. It does not, however, become part of the liturgy. In fact, meditation on the mysteries of the Rosary, by familiarizing the hearts and minds of the faithful with the mysteries of Christ, can be an excellent preparation for the celebration of those same mysteries in the liturgical action and can also become a continuing echo thereof. However, it is a mistake to recite the Rosary during the celebration of the liturgy, though unfortunately this practice still persists here and there.

49. The Rosary of the Blessed Virgin Mary, according to the tradition accepted by our predecessor St. Pius V and authoritatively taught by him, consists of various elements disposed in an organic fashion:

a) Contemplation in communion with Mary, of a series of *mysteries of salvation*, wisely distributed into three cycles. These mysteries express the joy of the messianic times, the salvific suffering of Christ and the glory of the Risen Lord which fills the Church. This contemplation by its very nature encourages practical reflection and provides stimulating norms for living.

b) The Lord's Prayer, as *Our Father*, which by reason of its immense value is at the basis of Christian prayer and ennobles that prayer in its various expressions.

c) The litany-like succession of the *Hail Mary*, which is made up of the angel's greeting to the Virgin (cf. Lk. 1:28), and of Elizabeth's greeting (cf. Lk. 1:42), followed by the ecclesial supplication, *Holy Mary*. The continued series of *Hail Mary's* is the special characteristic of the Rosary, and their number, in the full and typical number of one hundred and fifty, presents a certain analogy with the Psalter and is an element that goes back to the very origin of the exercise of piety. But this number, divided, according to a well-tried custom, into decades attached to the individual mysteries, is distributed in the three cycles already mentioned, thus giving rise to the Rosary of fifty *Hail Mary's* as we know it. This latter has entered into use as the normal measure of the pious exercise and as such has been adopted by popular piety and approved by papal authority, which also enriched it with numerous indulgences.

d) The doxology *Glory be to the Father* which, in conformity with an orientation common to Christian piety, concludes the prayer with the glorifying of God who is one and three, from whom, through whom and in whom all things have their being (cf. Rom. 11:36).

50. These are the elements of the Rosary. Each has its own particular character which, wisely understood and appreciated, should be reflected in the recitation in order that the Rosary may express all its richness and variety. Thus the recitation will be grave and suppliant during the Lord's Prayer, lyrical and full of praise during the tranquil succession of *Hail Mary's*, contemplative in the recollected meditation on the mysteries and full of adoration during the doxology. This applies to all the ways in which the Rosary is usually recited: privately, in intimate recollection with the Lord; in community, in the family or in groups of the faithful gathered together to ensure the special presence of the Lord (cf. Mt. 18:20); or publicly, in assemblies to which the ecclesial community is invited.

51. In recent times certain exercises of piety have been created which take their inspiration from the Rosary. Among such exercises we wish to draw attention to and recommend those which insert into the ordinary celebration of the word of God some elements of the Rosary, such as meditation on the mysteries and litany-like repetition of the angel's greeting to Mary. In this way these elements gain in importance, since they are found in the context of Bible readings, illustrated with a homily, accompanied by silent pauses and emphasized with song. We are happy to know that such practices have helped to promote a more complete understanding of the spiritual

riches of the Rosary itself and have served to restore esteem for its recitation among youth associations and movements.

52. We now desire, as a continuation of the thought of our predecessors, to recommend strongly the recitation of the family Rosary. The Second Vatican Council has pointed out how the family, the primary and vital cell of society, "shows itself to be the domestic sanctuary of the Church through the mutual affection of its members and the common prayer they offer to God."[115] The Christian family is thus seen to be a domestic Church[116] if its members, each according to his proper place and tasks, all together promote justice, practice works of mercy, devote themselves to helping their brethren, take part in the apostolate of the wider local community and play their part in its liturgical worship.[117] This will be all the more true if together they offer up prayers to God. If this element of common prayer were missing, the family would lack its very character as a domestic Church. Thus there must logically follow a concrete effort to reinstate communal prayer in family life if there is to be a restoration of the theological concept of the family as the domestic Church.

53. In accordance with the directives of the Council, the *Institutio Generalis de Liturgia Horarum* rightly numbers the family among the groups in which the Divine Office can suitably be celebrated in community: "It is fitting...that the family, as a domestic sanctuary of the Church, should not only offer prayers to God in common, but also, according to circumstances, should recite parts of the Liturgy of the Hours, in order to be more intimately linked with the Church."[118] No avenue should be left unexplored to ensure that this clear and practical recommendation finds within Christian families growing and joyful acceptance.

54. But there is no doubt that, after the celebration of the Liturgy of the Hours, the high point which family prayer can reach, the Rosary should be considered as one of the best and most efficacious prayers in common that the Christian family is invited to recite. We like to think, and sincerely hope, that when the family gathering becomes a time of prayer, the Rosary is a frequent and favored manner

of praying. We are well aware that the changed conditions of life today do not make family gatherings easy, and that even when such a gathering is possible many circumstances make it difficult to turn it into an occasion of prayer. There is no doubt of the difficulty. But it is characteristic of the Christian in his manner of life not to give in to circumstances but to overcome them, not to succumb but to make an effort. Families which want to live in full measure the vocation and spirituality proper to the Christian family must therefore devote all their energies to overcoming the pressures that hinder family gatherings and prayer in common.

55. In concluding these observations, which give proof of the concern and esteem which the Apostolic See has for the Rosary of the Blessed Virgin, we desire at the same time to recommend that this very worthy devotion should not be propagated in a way that is too one-sided or exclusive. The Rosary is an excellent prayer, but the faithful should feel serenely free in its regard. They should be drawn to its calm recitation by its intrinsic appeal.

Footnotes

Chapter 1

1.   The Holy Rosary, Daughters of St. Paul, Boston, MA, 1980, p. 285.
2.   Wilfred Lescher, O.P., St. Dominic and the Rosary, R&T Washbourne, London, Eng., 1902, p. 9.
3.   J. Proctor, O.P., The Rosary Guide, Kegan and Trubner & Co., London, Eng., 1901, p. 27.
4.   Ibid., p. 19.
5.   Ibid., p. 8.
6.   Ibid., p. 9.
7. The Holy Rosary, p. 47.
8. St. Dominic and the Rosary, p. 5.
9. The Holy Rosary, p. 72.
10. Ibid., p. 81.
11. Catholic Mind, Aug. 22, 1921, p. 219.
12. The Holy Rosary, p. 169.

Chapter 2

1.   John Rubba, O.P., St. Dominic Guzman, Founder of the Order of Preachers, p. 1.
2.   Catherine of Siena, The Dialogue, Paulist Press., New York, N.Y., 1980, p. 337.
3.   Gabriel Hardy, O.P., Rediscovering the Rosary, Veritas Publications, Dublin, Ireland, 1983, p. 9.
4.   St. Louis de Montfort, Secret of the Rosary, Tan Books and Publishers, Inc., Rockford, IL, 1984, p. 19.
5.   St. Dominic Guzman, Founder of the Order of Preachers, p. 12.
6.   Ibid., p. 9.
7.   John Rubba, O.P., The Dominicans-A Brief History, p. 13.
8.   Sister Assumpta O'Hanlon, O.P., Servant but Friend, Herder & co., London, Eng., 1954, p. 132.
9.   Catherine of Sienna, The Dialogue, p. 339.

10. St. Dominic Guzman - Founder of the Rosary, p. 25.

11. Sister Mary Jean Dorcy, O.P., St. Dominic, Tan Publishing, Rockford, IL, 1982, p. 144.

12. J. Proctor, O.P., The Rosary Guide, Kegan and Trebner & Co., London, Eng., 1901, p. 26.

13. Simon Tugwell, O.P., St. Dominic and the Order of Preachers, Dominican Publications, Dublin, Ireland, 1981, p. 15.

14. The Crown of Mary, Apostolate of the Rosary, New York, N.Y., 1935.

15. Servant but Friend, p. 63.

16. Confidence for the Future, Dominican Publication, Dublin, Ireland, 1982, p. 80.

17. Torchlites, Newsletter of the Dominican Laity, 1994, p. 3.

18. The Holy Rosary, Daughters of St. Paul, Boston, MA 1980, p. 50.

Chapter 3

1. John Paul II, Theotokos, Pauline Books, Boston, MA 2000, p. 199.

2. Ibid., p. 192.

3. Mark Tremeau, O.P., The Mystery of the Rosary, Catholic Publishing Co., New York, NY, 1982, p. 27.

4. John Paul II, Mother of the Redeemer, Pauline Books, Boston, MA, 1987, p. 6.

5. Mystery of the Rosary, p. 46.

6. St. Louis de Montfort, Secret of the Rosary, Tan Books and Publishing, Inc., Rockford, IL, 1984, p. 85.

7. Mystery of the Rosary, p. 49.

8. Paul VI, Marialis Cultus, Daughters of St. Paul, Boston, MA, 1982, p. 42.

9. Gabriel Harty, O.P., Riches of the Rosary, Veritas Publications, Dublin, 1997, p. 67.

10. Catholic World Report, Ignatius Press, Feb. 2001, San Francisco, CA, p. 8.

11. Confidence for the Future, Dominican Publication, Dublin, Ireland, 1982, p. 79.

12. Ibid., p. 79.

13. Jesus Living in Mary, Montfort Publication, Bayshore, NY, 1994, p. 1060.

14. J. Proctor, O.P., The Rosary Guide, Kegan and Trubner & Co., London, Eng., 1901, p. 86.

15. L'Osservatore Romano, Vatican City, May 20, 1991, p. 10.

16. Ibid., p. 1.

17. L'Osservatore Romano, Vatican City, Oct. 10, 1988, p. 10.

18. L'Osservatore Romano, Vatican City, Oct. 4, 1995, p. 8.

19. John Paul II, The Role of the Christian Family in the Modern World, Daughters of St. Paul, Boston, MA, 1981, p. 89.

20. <u>Jesus Living in Mary</u>, Montfort Publications, Bayshore, NY, 1994, p. 1059.

21. Ibid., p. 1064.

22. Ibid., p. 1059.

23. <u>Mystery of the Rosary</u>, p. 62.

24. <u>L'Osservatore Romano</u>, June 8, 1987, p. 2.

25. <u>L'Osservatore Romano</u>, May 5, 1999, p. 1.

26. Ibid., p. 1.

27. Ibid., p. 4.

28. <u>L'Osservatore Romano</u>, May 28, 1990, p. 9.

29. Ibid., p. 9.

30. <u>Bartolo Longo</u>, Oct. 1920, p. 39.

31. <u>Bartolo Longo - At the Service of God & Man</u>, Pontifical Shrine of Pompei, Pompei, Italy, 1993, p. 11.

32. Ibid., p. 11.

33. Gennaro Auletta, <u>Shrine of Pompei</u>, Pompei, Italy, 1987, p. 182.

34. <u>L'Osservatore Romano</u>, Nov. 3, 1980, p. 1.

Chapter 4

1. <u>L'Osservatore Romano</u>, Vatican City, May 18, 1987, p. 24.

2. Andre Fossard, <u>"Be Not Afraid"</u>, St. Martin's Press, New York, NY, 1982, p. 125.

3. John Paul II, <u>This is Your Mother</u>, St. Paul Publications, Athlow, Ireland, 1981, p. 160.

4. John Paul II, <u>Crossing the Threshold of Hope</u>, Random House and Alfred Knoph, New York, NY, 1994, p. 142.

5. <u>L'Osservatore Romano</u>, Jan. 10, 2001, p. 7.

6. <u>L'Osservatore Romano</u>, June 18, 1997, p. 11.

7. John Paul II, <u>This is Your Mother</u>, St. Paul Publications, Athlow, Ireland, 1981, pp. 17-18.

8. <u>Crossing the Threshold of Hope</u>, p. 214.

9. John Paul II, <u>A Year with Mary</u>, Catholic Publishing Co., New York, NY, 1986, p. 220.

10. <u>L'Osservatore Romano</u>, June 18, 1997, p. 11.

11. <u>L'Osservatore Romano</u>, Oct. 12, 1987, p. 18.

12. <u>Soul Magazine</u>, Sept. - Oct. 2000, Blue Army, Washington, NJ, p. 23.

13. Fr. Jose Freire, <u>Fatima Pilgrim</u>, Sanctuary of Fatima, 1985, p. 37.

14. <u>L'Osservatore Romano</u>, May 17, 1982, p. 3.

15. <u>L'Osservatore Romano</u>, May 18, 1987, p. 24.

16. <u>L'Osservatore Romano</u>, May 20, 1991, p. 10.

17. <u>Soul Magazine</u>, p. 2.

18. <u>L'Osservatore Romano</u>, Nov. 1, 1998, p. 2.

19. L'Osservatore Romano, June 7, 1982, p. 1.

20. L'Osservatore Romano, Oct. 13, 1999, p. 1.

21. L'Osservatore Romano, Oct. 11, 2000, p. 1.

22. L'Osservatore Romano, Jan. 10, 2001, p. 11.

23. John Paul II, A Year with Mary, Catholic Publishing Co., New York, NY, 1986, p. 228.

24. L'Osservatore Romano, March 14, 2001, p. 1.

Chapter 5

1. Prayer and Devotions from John Paul II, Viking Books, New York, NY, 1994, p. 192.

2. Ibid., p. 194.

3. L'Osservatore Romano, Vatican City, May 13, 1982, p. 3.

4. John De Marchi, I.M.C., Fatima, The Full Message, AMI Press, Washington, NJ, 1986, p. 134.

5. Fr. Robert Fox, Fatima Today, Christendom College Publications, Front Royal, VA, 1983, p. 174.

6. Fatima, The Full Message, p. 245.

7. Francis Johnson, The Great Sign, Tan Books & Publishing, Inc., Rockford, IL, 1980, p. 108.

8. Ibid., p. 4.

9. Ibid., p. 120.

10. Boundless Gift - John Paul II, OFICYNA, Wydawnicza, Krakow, Poland, 1997, p. 48.

11. L'Osservatore Romano, April 4, 2001, p. 5.

12. L'Osservatore Romano, May 17, 2000, p. 3.

13. Ibid., p. 2.

14. Ibid., p. 2.

15. Ibid., p. 2.

16. Fr. Robert Fox, The Intimate Life of Sister Lucia, Fatima Family Apostolate, Alexandria, SD, 2001, p. 325.

17. The Pope Speaks, Nov/Dec 2000, Sunday Visitor, Hungington, IN, p. 360.

18. Ibid., p. 374.

19. Ibid., p. 374.

20. Ibid., p. 375.

21. Ibid., p. 376.

22. Ibid., p. 377-78.

23. John Paul II, Crossing the Threshold of Hope, Random House, NY, NY, 1994, p. 211.

Chapter 6

1. Reginald Garrigou-Lagrange, O. P., <u>Mother of the Savior</u>, B. Herder Co., St. Louis, MO, 1959, p. 255.

2. Archibishop Finbar Ryan, O.P., <u>Our Lady of Fatima</u>, Browne and Nolan, Dublin, Ireland, 1943, p. 99.

3. Marc Tremeau, O.P., <u>The Mystery of the Rosary</u>, Catholic Publishing Co., New York, NY, 1982, p. 9.

4. <u>The Holy Rosary</u>, Daughters of St. Paul, Boston, MA, 1980, p. 49.

5. Ibid., p. 169.

6. <u>The Mystery of the Rosary</u>, p. 40.

7. Ibid., p. 42.

8. Ibid., p. 41.

9. Ibid., p. 274-276.

10. <u>Catechism of the Catholic Church</u>, Ligouri Publications, Ligouri, MO, 1994, p. 650.

11. Reginald Coffey, O.P., <u>The Man from Rocca Sicca</u>, Bruce Publishing, Milwaukee, WI, 1942, p. 140.

12. <u>Catherine of Siena - The Dialogue</u>, Paulist Press, New York, NY, 1980, p. 339.

13. <u>Letter of Paul VI for Seventh Centenary of St. Thomas Aquinas</u>, Order of Friars Preachers, Rome, Italy, 1975.

Chapter 8

1. Fr. E.C. McEniry, O.P., <u>St. Thomas Aquinas Meditations for Every Day</u>, Long College Book Co., Columbus, OH, 1951, p. 22-23.

2. Ibid., p. 359-360.

3. <u>The Sixteen Documents of Vatican II</u>, St. Paul Editions, Boston, MA, p. 171.

4. Ibid., p. 377.

Chapter 9

1. Fr. E.C. McEniry, O.P., p. 298-299.

2. Ibid., p. 363-364.

3. <u>Dogmatic Constitution on the Church: Lumen Gentium</u>, St. Paul Editions, Boston, MA, 1964, p. 54.

Chapter 10

1. Fr. E.C. McEniry, O.P., p. 47-48.

2. Ibid., p. 41-42.

3. Ibid., p. 58-59.
4. Ibid., p. 57-58.
5. Ibid., p. 382-383.
6. Ibid., p. 386-387.
7. Pope John Paul II, <u>Sign of Contradiction</u>, Seabury Press, New York, NY, 1979, p. 40.

Chapter 11

1. Fr. E.C. McEniry, O.P., p. 92-93.
2. Ibid., p. 91.
3. Ibid., p. 370-371.
4. Pope John Paul II, <u>Sign of Contradiction</u>, p. 41.

Chapter 12

1. Fr. E.C. McEniry, O.P., p. 62-62.
2. Ibid., p. 367-368.

Chapter 13

1. Fr. E.C. McEniry, O.P., p. 127-128.
2. Ibid., p. 373-374.
3. Ibid., p. 375-377.
4. Ibid., p. 88-89.
5. Ibid., p. 378-379.
6. Ibid., p. 251.
7. <u>The Sixteen Documents of Vatican II</u>, p. 20.
8. Pope John Paul II, <u>Sign of Contradiction</u>, p. 74.

Chapter 14

1. Fr. E.C. McEniry, O.P., p. 142-143.
2. Ibid., p. 372-373.
3. Pope John Paul II, <u>Sign of Contradiction</u>, p. 75.

Chapter 15

1. Fr. Reginald Garrigou-Lagrange, O.P., <u>Love of God</u>, B. Herder Co., St. Louis, MO, 1951, p. 440.
2. Fr. E.C. McEniry, O.P., p. 397-398.
3. Pope John Paul II, <u>Sign of Contradiction</u>, p. 76.

4. Ibid., p. 77.

Chapter 16

1. Fr. Reginald Garrigou-Lagrange, O.P., <u>Love of God</u>, p. 422.
2. Ibid., p. 422-423.
3. Ibid., p. 423.
4. Ibid., p. 425.
5. Fr. E.C. McEniry, O.P., p. 370-371.
6. Pope John Paul II, <u>Sign of Contradiction</u>, p. 77-78.

Chapter 17

1. Fr. Reginald Garrigou-Lagrange, O.P., <u>Love of God</u>, p. 428.
2. Ibid., p. 430.
3. Ibid., p. 431-432.
4. Ibid., p. 433.
5. Fr. E.C. McEniry, O.P., p. 399-400.
6. <u>Dogmatic Constitutions on the Church</u>, p. 57.

Chapter 18

1. Fr. E.C. McEniry, O.P., p. 201-202.
2. Ibid., p. 203-204.
3. Ibid., p. 205-206.
4. Ibid., p. 211-212.
5. Ibid., p. 436-437.
6. Pope John Paul II, <u>Sign of Contradiction</u>, p. 110.

Chapter 19

1. Fr. E.C. McEniry, O.P., p. 252-253.
2. Ibid., p. 255.
3. Ibid., p. 362-363.

Chapter 20

1. Fr. E.C. McEniry, O.P., p. 262.
2. Ibid., p. 264-266.
3. Ibid., p. 270-271.
4. Ibid., p. 232-233.
5. <u>Dogmatic Constitutions on the Church</u>, p. 57.

6. Pope John Paul II, Redeemer of Man, USCC, Washington, D.C., 1979, p. 71.

Chapter 21

1. Fr. E.C. McEniry, O.P., p. 323-324.
2. Ibid., p. 59.
3. Dogmatic Constitutions on the Church, p. 58.
4. Pope John Paul II, A Year with Mary, p. 185.

Chapter 22

1. Fr. Reginald Garrigou-Lagrange, O.P., Love of God, p. 447.
2. Ibid., p. 447.
3. John Paul II, Theotokas, Pauline Books, Boston, MA, 2000, pp. 210-211.

Chapter 23

1. St. Louis de Montfort, p. 61.
2. Ibid., p. 34.
3. Catechism of the Catholic Church, Liguori Publications, Liguori, MO, 1994, p. 662.
4. Ibid., p. 662.
5. St. Louis de Montfort, p. 42.
6. Ibid., p. 46.
7. God Alone, Montfort Publications, Bay Shore, NY, 1995, p. 369.
8. Ibid., p. 370.
9. J. Augustine Di Noia, O.P., Gabriel O'Donnell, O.P., Romanus Cessario, O.P., Peter Cameron, O.P., The Love That Never Ends, Our Sunday Visitor, Huntington, IN, 1996, p. 137.
10. In the Little Way of St. Teresa of Lisieux, Catholic Truth Society, London, England, 1973, p. 21.
11. St. Thomas Aquinas, Catechetical Instructions of St. Thomas Aquinas, Sinag-Tala Publishers, Inc., Manila, Philippines, p. 200-201.
12. Ibid., p. 203-211.

Chapter 24

1. God Alone, Montfort Publications, Bay Shore, NY, 1995, p. 197.
2. Ibid., p. 196.
3. Valentine Long, O.F.M., The Mother of God, Franciscan Herald Press, Chicago, IL, 1976, p. 128.
4. Peter Lappin, First Lady of the World, Don Bosco Publications, New Roch-

elle, NY, 1988, p. 174.
5. St. Louis de Montfort, p. 62.
6. The Holy Rosary, Daughters of St. Paul, Boston, MA, 1980, p. 137.
7. St. Louis de Montfort, p. 97.

Bibliography

Aquinas, St. Thomas, <u>The Catechetical Instructions of St. Thomas Aquinas</u>, Sinag-Tala Publishers, Manila, Philippines.

Coffey, O.P., Reginald M., <u>The Man from Rocca Sicca</u>, Bruce Publishing Co., Milwaukee, WI, 1942.

De Marchi, I.M.C., John, <u>Fatima, The Full Story</u>, AMI Press, Inc., Washington, NJ, 1986.

De Montfort, St. Louis, <u>The Secret of the Rosary</u>, Tan Publishers, Rockford, IL, 1984.

<u>Dogmatic Constitution on the Church</u>, St. Paul Editions, Boston, MA, 1964.

Fox., Rev. Robert, <u>Rediscovering Fatima</u>, Our Sunday Visitor, Hungington, IN, 1982.

Fox., Rev. Robert, <u>Fatima Today</u>, Christendom Publications, Front Royal, VA, 1983.

Garrigou-Lagrange, O.P., Reginald, <u>Love of God</u>, B. Herder Do., St. Louis, MO, 1951.

Garrigou-Lagrange, O.P., Reginald, <u>Mother of the Savior</u>, B. Herder Co., St. Louis, MO, 1959.

Hardy, O.P., Gabriel, <u>Rediscovering the Rosary</u>, Veritas Publications, Dublin, Ireland, 1979.

Hardy, O.P., Gabriel, <u>Riches of the Rosary</u>, Veritas Publications, Dublin, Ireland, 1997.

John Paul II, <u>A Year with Mary</u>, Catholic Book Publishing, New York, NY, 1986.
John Paul II, Sign of Contradiction, The Seabury Press, New York, NY, 1979.

Lescher, O.P., Wilfred, <u>St. Dominic and the Rosary</u>, Rt. Washbourne, London, Eng., 1902.

Martins, S.J., Antonio, <u>Fatima and Our Salvation</u>, Augustine Publishing Co., Chulmeigh, England, 1985.

McEniry, O.P., E.C., <u>St. Thomas Aquinas Meditations</u>, Long's College Book Co., Columbus, OH, 1951.

<u>The Holy Rosary</u>, Daughters of St. Paul, Boston, MA, 1980.

<u>The Sixteen Documents of Vatican II</u>, Daughters of St. Paul, Boston, MA.

Tremeau, O.P., Mark, <u>The Mystery of the Rosary</u>, Catholic Book Publishing Co., New York, NY, 1982.

Weisheipl, O.P., James A., <u>Friar Thomas D'Aquino - His Life, Thought, and Work</u>, Doubleday & Company, Garden City, NY, 1974.